Photo Credit:
Artwork by Malika Ayyubi, "A Nostalgic Staircase"

ISBN: 978-1-7373061-1-5

First Edition February 2023
ISBN: 978-1-7373061-1-5

Printed in the United States of America.
Library of Congress Cataloging-in-Publication Data
TBD

Published and Distributed by:
Adhwaq Publishing
616 Georgetown Parkway
Fenton, MI 48430
Email : publishing@adhwaqcenter.org
Web: https://www.adhwaqcenter.org

Contents

Foreword
By Prof. Rudolph Bilal Ware

Dr. Ali Hussain has written a manifesto for the Muslim creative—and much more than this. *A Nostalgic Remembrance* flows from the material to the metaphysical, all the while remaining rooted in an ontology of *zikr*, remembrance of the Divine. This most quintessentially Islamic of devotional practices has—in this spiritually impoverished age—come to be narrowly associated with the Sufi mystical tradition.

Here, Hussain restores *Divine remembrance* to its rightful place at the core of *all creative activity*. The Qur'an, of course, describes itself as *zikr* so it is most fitting that the Qur'an is at the heart of this book's *nostalgic remembrance*. Islam's Holy Writ is always there as a memory inspiring reflection and deep longing for reunion and transcendence. Dr. Hussain is also a *Hafiz*— meaning he can recite the entire Qur'an from memory in Arabic. In reading this book, it is clear not only does the author know the Qur'an by heart, but it is close to his heart as well.

But above all it is the stunningly eclectic range of the sources that Hussain uses to engage Qur'anic concepts that makes this a *universal* contribution to the philosophy of the arts. Putting Hemingway in dialogue with Ghazali, Shakespeare with Langston Hughes, Dr. Hussain dances with the dead, reviving them like the true Christ that was the subject of his Ph.D. dissertation in Islamic studies.

Gliding from *Star Wars*, to the Qur'anic cosmology of angels, to Maya Angelou, this is above all a *moving remembrance*. This book is constantly flowing from one world into another, one temporality into the next. In reading the book, time itself is lost like a dervish in a trance. The chapters speed past, in part because of the beauty and clarity of the writing, but also because of its clear and systematic organization.

Beginning with what the Qur'an teaches us about storytelling and creativity, we are first reminded that our very existence is the expressive art of a singular creative Entity, and that each artist is indeed art as well. The first half of the book functions in this way like a universal treatise on creativity before moving to take on writing, visual, auditory and movement arts.

I should add that I personally found the reading of this book deeply gratifying as a poet, musician, and academic. I am perhaps best known as the author of *The Walking Qur'an*, a scholarly study of textual embodiment in the Islamic tradition. One of the most frequently misunderstood elements of that tradition—for those within and without Islam—is that it is a backwards-looking tradition focused narrowly on conservation and preservation.

Nothing—I have argued—could be further from the Truth. The Islamic tradition has always celebrated innovation and creativity, but it has insisted that *mastery* precede improvisation. As a *hafiz* and scholar, an author and artist, Dr. Ali Hussain has demonstrated true mastery and creativity in the composition of this work. There is great benefit here for all who seek to understand the spiritual core of creation.

Dr. Rudolph Bilal Ware is a specialist on Africa and Islam. He earned his Ph.D. in history in 2004 from the University of Pennsylvania where he was trained in African History, African-American History, and Islamic Intellectual History. He is currently an associate professor in the Department of History at the University of California-Santa Barbara, and the founder and director of the Initiative for the Study of Race, Religion, and Revolution (ISRRAR). Dr. Ware has published numerous books and articles on Islamic knowledge, social justice, Sufi poetry, and anticolonial resistance. He is also a speaker, public intellectual, poet, emcee, producer and co-founder of the Hip Hop group *Slum Prophecy*.

Preface

"Listen to the reed-flute,
how it laments separation from the reed-bed"
– Rumi, *Mathnawi*

The Egyptian novelist Naguib Mahfouz wrote in his Nobel prize acceptance letter: "I am a child born from the marriage of two civilizations: ancient Egyptian and Islamic." I, on the other hand, am born at the intersection of several waves: Iraqi, Egyptian, Islamic, and American. That diverse soil, life experiences, and journeys have delivered me to this juncture and book that I gift to you, an intrigued reader.

Like a good writer – or perhaps not – I am composing this preface only after completing this entire work. In a way, I am following the Sufi sense of temporality, where time proceeds like a cycle, and the end must embrace the beginning. The pages you find here are the end of such a turn and beginning of a return. I have also contemplated the writing of this work numerous times over the past decade, but the motivation was never truly there. It is only when it became a recurrent visitor that I took the plunge and began righting the wrong of delaying this project.

I was born to a family of artists. My mother is a painter and interior decorator, father a photographer, brother an architect, and sister a pottery maker. The earliest memories I have from my childhood, which I spent in diaspora and migration, is my family's artwork. It's imprinted in memory, and stands as a soothing meditation amidst other images, sounds, and movements that have to do with war and exile.

I was almost seven years old when the First Gulf War enveloped Baghdad. It took the entire city by surprise, including the buildings that did not expect to be mutilated on a fateful night. As we drove through the streets of Baghdad the day after the first bombing, we saw the intestines of architecture and people on the streets, spilling memories and privacy of its residents. Some of these buildings even housed friends that we had visited just a week prior.

This is perhaps why my memory of Iraq is blurred as pertaining to people, yet much clearer surrounding buildings. Architecture, and all art by extension, is a self-edifying journal; it chronicles the memories of people in silence, as they live obliviously expecting today to last forever, and tomorrow to be even further than eternity. But art understands the importance of such naïve hope; it stores these memories for an uncertain future.

I will have recourse to the details of the war later in this book; for now, you should know that after the assault on Iraq my father left for Jordan to start a new life for his family. We stayed behind for a few years, <u>a part</u> of us home and another ready to <u>depart</u>. Of course, the real Iraq had already left. Even electricity had migrated, leaving behind hours upon hours of darkness. The breezes of Baghdad no longer carried the smell of jasmine but bullets and blood. We did not choose to leave, but it seems we had overstayed our welcome.

Iraqi artists had long since become accustomed to bullets and blood and learned how to embrace it in their work. I pay homage here to the poet Ahmad Matar whose short work *Qalam Rasas* plays with the twin meanings of *rasas* (bullet and pencil):

> The doctor measured my pulse
> "Is the pain here?" … "Yes!"
> "The doctor incised with his knife
> My shirt's pocket and took out a pen."
> The doctor tilted his head and smiled:
> "It is nothing but a pen!"
> "No dear sir. This is a hand and tongue."
> "A bullet and blood"
> "And a lonely crime, walking barefoot!"

War and revolution are as common as bread in the Middle East: necessary and expensive. And if it were not for two traits that are common to all Arabs, the arts and a sense of humor, they would have perished long ago.

After my father left Iraq for Jordan, in those few years before we followed him, away from our home towards another across the desert, it was my mother's friends from the Iraqi television, mostly actors, who visited us regularly at my grandmother's house. Many of them hugged me and "played the role of the father" in his absence. This was but one of many moments, turned into a memory with the passing of time, where art and artists mended the wounds of war.

A few years ago, I came across a video of an Iraqi actor who was very well known during my childhood. He was on his deathbed as one of his friends – another actor – was visiting him. When he saw his friend sick and bedridden, he exclaimed his dismay using a well-known Iraqi expression: *sudug chidhib*!? (Truth or lie?), which roughly translates to: "How is this possible? How has our condition become like this?" It is a fairly common proverb that can be used to make sense of both trivial problems and far more serious turn of events.

Some weeks after watching this video, I was standing in line at a Dollar store, watching two Iraqi men converse. One was asking the other if he had a $100 bill. Responding negatively, the first made the same exclamation: *sudug chidhib*. Suddenly, the walls of the store transformed, and I was back in Baghdad. This simple expression communicating itself to me through two incidents was no coincidence, but a co-incidence.

It was Iraq itself speaking to me: "Look what happened to your homeland!" Between actors passing away that had brought my childhood to life and young Iraqis alive today who do not have a $100 bill, I suddenly came to terms with the resilience of my people. They teach me that suffering itself can be a tool in our redemption. From this epiphany, I was gifted a poem to write about the actors and two young men at the Dollar store, in exchange for the fact that I keep this memory alive through the bullet of the pen and blood of my memories.

After moving and living in Jordan for six years, a transitory period prior to migrating across the ocean to America, a different type of art kept me company and alleviated the anxiety of learning a new culture and how to make friends. That definitive period of my childhood is colored by galleries of my father's photography, mother's paintings, visiting my sister's pottery workshop, and seeing my brother's architectural models at his university fair.

For me personally, it was my exposure to American cinema through films like *Edward Scissorhands*, *Heart and Soul*, and prior to that in Baghdad, Tim Burton's *Batman* and James Cameron's *Terminator 2*, all of which was a safe space for me to journey into when physical reality seemed too much to handle. But alongside film, it was also video games that provided much solace. Traveling into a virtual world where you can play a story to its resolution can bring much hope to our own unfinished tales.

This exposure to the American arts had heightened my desire to visit the United States. In 1997, when we finally migrated to America, it was not exactly as Hollywood had portrayed, but not that far off the mark; if only you knew where and how to look. Just as I had troubles making friends when I first came to Jordan, I found myself in a similar position in Michigan. I had become Edward Scissorhands, secluded with the proverbial scissors of my foreign culture that singled me out regularly in crowds.

It was not until sophomore year in high school, when I met my English teacher and lifetime mentor Ryan Goble, that things improved drastically. It was his first-year teaching, and we were his inaugural class. Coming with an undergraduate degree in English and screenplay writing certificate from UCLA, Ryan believed – and still does – in teaching English using popular culture. Beethoven's *Ode to Joy* and *Moonlight Sonata* was the only Western music I knew in Jordan. All of a sudden, in the span of a few months, I was exposed to the Beatles, Spike Lee, and the Manhattan project.

There is much content that Goble had taught us, even more so that he showed us. This includes trips to the Rock and Roll Hall of Fame, Chicago Institute of the Arts Museum, Hollywood, and New York among others. However, the most important lesson that remains with me today, even shaping the very contours of this book, is his method: making connections across disciplines and crafts to decipher new knowledge. Ryan is a Renaissance man who was teaching us an ancient way of learning.

I was dealing with my own inner struggles at the time, having only migrated to the United States some two years prior and still learning how to express myself both vocally and in writing using English. Thus, I did not truly appreciate what this teacher had unfolded before me and my other classmates. Nevertheless, I have reached the great realization that such unawareness is sometimes bliss. As Sufi mystics teach, some experiences might make sense immediately, others will take years to <u>foment</u> before they <u>ferment</u>.

It was also my exposure, infatuation, and obsession with professional wrestling during high school that was a rite of passage and introduced me to American culture in the most raw and gritty form possible. However, it was not until many years later that I understood the mystical and metaphysical significance of this artform: why was I was so drawn to it?

Why did I dress and speak like my favorite characters? What was the significance of calling the wrestling ring a 'squared circle'?

After two field trips, first to Hollywood where we met the late Robin Williams, and New York where we visited the late William Goldman, we had such a somber realization that something great was coming to an end. And so, where do we go from here? This feeling would cascade like an avalanche after graduating from high school. Each of us went our separate way, yet still tried to make sense of what had transpired over the past few years.

My own journey was still awaiting a great synthesis. Some pieces were missing that had not yet made themselves known. In college, I studied Mathematics and Computer Science, eventually completing a masters in Artificial Intelligence, all with the hope of becoming a video game designer. I wanted to tell stories; that was my impetus. However, fate redirected me after ten years where I found myself applying to doctoral programs in the humanities to study the notion of intelligence in Islamic mysticism, also known as Sufism.

From April 2011 to April 2012, I studied religiously – no pun intended – hoping to be accepted in a religious studies program. It was during this period that I was exposed to the writings of the Sufi saint Ibn al-ʿArabi (d. 1240) whose teachings accompany us in this book. It was during this studious year that I also found myself writing creatively, specifically in Arabic. I was not composing essays to just prove to universities that I could read and write in my native tongue. Rather, something greater was <u>materializing</u> and <u>matriculating</u>.

Prior to discussing that, I should mention that my initial impetus for obtaining a PhD in Islamic studies was not sincere. I had my faith reborn in America in the early 2000s, transitioning from an illiterate phase where I did not know the different sects, despite being born a sushi – half Sunni and half Shi'i Muslim – to eventually becoming an education chair at my local mosque and being exposed to a rather spiritually-dead flavor of Islam. Later, in 2008, I somehow stumbled upon Sufism.

Prior to that, in 2007, it was the TV show *Lost* that saved me from spiritually-dead Islam. I was taken by the storytelling, mythology, depth, and kept telling myself: "If I am feeling more spiritually uplifted watching this show for one hour than going to that mosque for two years, something is wrong." I was in no way disenchanted by my faith, but rather enchanted and felt more aware of the sacredness of art. I tasted the ability of film to convey spiritual realities at such a visceral and emotional level that mainstream religious discourse had lacked immensely.

My first introduction to Sufism was scholastic; not yet a complete transition to *dhawq*-oriented (taste) mysticism. It was bookish and rational, but nevertheless a good intermediary period. And herein comes my reason for pursuing a doctoral degree in Islamic studies: I sought legitimization by a community of faith that otherwise – I felt – would not accept my opinion. Little did I know that the only thing worse than not having any Islamic education at all is having an academic degree in Islamic studies without an *ijaza* (religious license) from a seminary.

But all was well because art and creativity had other plans. Ibn al-ʿArabi had filled all sorts of gaps in my heart. Most important among which is that he appeared to provide the metaphysical foundations for what Ryan Goble had tried to do in high school, and much more. For the Sufi mystic, who is thoroughly an emanationist and Neoplatonist, all things physical are rooted in the spiritual realm. More than that, multiple disparate entities in our world can actually have a common spiritual ancestor.

This gave voice to many of my eccentricities that I had experienced throughout my life. My exposure to Arabic *maqam* (modal) music at a young age in Jordan and weeping after hearing the *adhan* (call to prayer) being chanted in a somber melody, then later learning about these different modalities and the feelings they evoke was suddenly making sense in the context of my nostalgia for a childhood that I like to describe as 'orphaned of a motherland'.

I began to appreciate my infatuation with professional wrestling as a love for mythology, the most sacred of crafts in human history. The 'squared circle' emerged as the perfect allegory for the perplexity inherent in human imagination and our desire to make sense of opposites like good vs. evil, light vs. darkness, and existence vs. non-existence. I also appreciated the power of artwork like the show *Lost* in its ability to convey and communicate the unseen much more eloquently than rational legalism or dialectical theology.

Much more importantly than the content of Ibn al-ʿArabi's teachings, it was his style and method. His ability to 'make connections where none seem possible or exist' <u>painted</u> a portrait in my mind of an artist-saint. He had <u>drawn</u> the ire of several Muslim scholars during his time – and even now – who simply could not understand what he experienced of reality or why it was so drastically different than theirs. To them, he was a madman who had perceived meanings in the Qurʾan that were simply not there.

But I understood that he was reading scripture just as an artist would look at a painting, not expecting a direct answer but instead wondering how it speaks to their emotions and feelings. Perhaps nothing displays this Sufi mystic's creative spirit more than his innovative etymology, whereby he finds connections between Arabic words that grammar does not believe should be made. However, his vision makes perfect sense once you take affairs back to the spirit, as he does.

I finished my PhD in 2018, writing a dissertation on the presence of Jesus in Ibn al-ʿArabi's writings. But at the end of that six-year journey, I did not find myself an academic as much an artist. By that time, I had already published my first collection of essays and poetic reflections *Mystical Musings of a Contemporary Dervish* and was assiduously working on my imaginative autobiography. In 2017, I began learning the oud, my musical companion that beautifully synthesized my love for Arabic music and the Qurʾan.

I was also thinking seriously about the spiritual dimensions of the creative process through the lens of Ibn al-ʿArabi. His elaborations upon *khayal* (imagination), the liminal nature of the universe, and the *hayra* (perplexity) inherent in all things resonated with me immensely. But what enchanted the entire process is that I found myself, like Ryan Goble and Ibn al-ʿArabi himself, involuntarily forging connections everywhere. Here is a statement by Picasso that sounds like something the Sufi mystic might say. Here is another by Yoda that I could almost find verbatim in the Qurʾan.

Although many Muslim scholars admonished me for comparing profane culture with sacred scripture, while academics criticized my proclivity to 'make connections where none seem possible or exist', I did not care. I had found my craft. I was not only seeking to be a poet, musician, photographer, or preacher. Instead, I was hoping to reside at the intersection. I wanted to be the saint described in T.S. Eliot's "Dry Salvages", the one who resides: "At the intersection of the timeless with time."

Perhaps that is because I myself, as mentioned above, was born at such a liminal interstice, at the meeting point of so many cultural, linguistic, and civilizational waves. Now, it is clear to me that the path forward was what has transpired before you in the book. This is a journey that began in 2014 and culminated in this form. In that year, I wrote my first intellectual argument for integrating Sufi metaphysics with contemporary culture in a paper titled: "The Light of the Blessed Tree: Islam's Intellectual Imperative in Modernity".

Since then, I have been blessed to teach numerous onsite and online retreats on the sacred dimensions of the creative process, spirituality of

Star Wars, video games, Khalil Gibran, and various workshops discussing my own poetry and music. As I mentioned in the beginning, the idea of this book was materializing through the years, awaiting other teaching and learning experiences that were needed for a synthesis to emerge in ink on paper.

So, what exactly is this book about? It is a deep journey into the metaphysics of the creative process through the teachings of Ibn al-ʿArabi and other Sufi mystics. I come to this project with all the life experiences I have mentioned in the preceding pages and a principle that I have learned and continue to apply in my life: *to make connections where none seem possible or exist.* This is the first definition of the creative process I would like us to consider in the coming chapters, alongside the second: *to translate the ineffable into the tangible.*

The reason why I have chosen to host Sufi metaphysics and creativity together is because I live with the deep conviction that the mystical experience is identical to the creative process. Hence, I have formulated these twin definitions of creativity to guide us through this book: the first pertains, first and foremost, to art but is also central to the mystical experience. Meanwhile, the second is clearly visible in the mystical experience but can also be gleaned in creativity.

I have divided the book into two sections, each consisting of five chapters. The first part focuses on metaphysical foundations that apply to all crafts. Chapter one, "Following the Traces: On Storytelling", discusses the importance of narrative weaving as a sacred craft for humanity, with immense consequences on the wellbeing of the individual and society. Here, Ibn al-ʿArabi shows us how storytelling and myth weaving is a Christic inheritance and the highest form of divine flattery.

In chapter two, "The Hidden Treasure: On the Creative Process", we take a journey through an *athar* (narration) central in Sufism where God describes the process of creation as an unfolding hidden treasure, from an initial love to expansive knowledge. We look at the creative process as a five-stage journey that parallels the phases of divine creation and likewise mirrors the five levels of being, a concept that can be found in the teachings of the school of Ibn al-ʿArabi.

In chapter three, "*Al-Haqiqa al-Muhammadiyya*: On Artist as Art", I posit the primordial light of the prophet Muhammad ﷺ as the ethereal matter of creative inspiration, the creative process itself, artist and art, all at once. We discuss the sage-artist as an instance and mirror of *al-insan al-kamil al-tamm* (the perfect and complete human), he or she who beautifully <u>reflects</u> and <u>refracts</u>, through the mirror of their body, soul, and spirit the divine names and attributes.

In chapter four, "The In-Between: On Imagination and Paradox", we venture into the most significant contributions of Ibn al-ʿArabi central to the creative process, pertaining to the contours of human and divine imagination, as well as the intimate paradox and perplexity that is inherent in creativity and art. The Sufi mystic shows us how dreams and creativity are not mere mental constructs but a reality that permeates our entire existence. Not only is imagination a self-standing realm, but also extends the entire cosmos as a creative apparition.

"*Sharīʿa* of the Craft: On the Path to *Haqiqa*", the last chapter in part one tries to outline a way forward for mastering crafts through the lens of Sufism, specifically the three stages of *shariʿa* (law/rules), *tariqa* (path), and *haqiqa* (reality). Here, we <u>adopt</u> and <u>adapt</u> another paradigm by the Malian sage Tierno Taal who delineated three states of faith: solid, liquid, and gas. This chapter truly brings together the previous sections in a holistic vision of the artist-sage as a master of artform(s) who has reached the summit and sings the siren song to guide others along the way.

Part two focuses on different genres of art, beginning with chapter five, "Memories in Ink: On the Written Arts". Here, we look at the craft of translation. I begin with my own journey as a first-generation Arab immigrant who writes in both, Arabic and English, often hosting these two languages in <u>bilingual</u> meetings, all the while <u>lingering</u> in-between, as a performative <u>act</u> to <u>reenact</u> my own migration in childhood.

In chapter six, "The Dye of God: On the Visual Arts", I look at the crafts of painting, sculpture, and architecture as metaphors that allude to the significance of reading not only the body, grammar or prose of art, but more importantly its spirit and poetry. I tether this conversation to the previous chapter on the written arts to see how reading the texture and memories of a novel might present itself in the visual arts.

In chapter seven, "The *Sawt Sarmad*: On the Auditory Arts", we envision the musical instrument as a wooden sage who teaches the musician the importance of annihilation and being an empty channel. This to allow the breath of the divine musician to pass through, uninterrupted and uncontained. As in the previous chapter, we continue to thread our conversation to prior sections, in an attempt to see what annihilation means for a writer or painter, as well as how reading the spirit of a craft manifests in the word of music.

In chapter eight, "The Reel of Reality: On the Moving Arts", we look at theater and film as a sacred synthesis of the written, visual, and auditory crafts. Here, we learn from sages like Sir Michael Caine, Al Pacino, and Steven Spielberg about the contours of their summits, what it says about the creative process and – more importantly – what it unveils about the human condition. This is because this book, as mentioned, begins from the premise that the mystical experience mirrors the creative process. To this we also add the dimension: what it means to be human.

In chapter nine, "*Ma'rifa* and *'Urf*: On Society and Mythology", we expand our conversation from the individual to society and community. There, I take the opportunity to offer some social critique of trends surrounding the arts and creativity in our society generally and my American Muslim community specifically. Although I address many points to my coreligionists, I hope that my non-Muslim readers will also be able to relate to this section's overarching narrative.

In the final concluding chapter, I offer some final remarks on what this book tries to accomplish, reiterating some of the points found here, as well as setting the frontier for where I hope the conversation goes therefrom. I consider this endeavor a work of art about art. Like any artist who plans for their painting, novel, or musical composition, I am also hopeful that this book will have an expansive life among readers.

I would now like to highlight some of my stylistic choices in this work. I regard this book no differently than my poems in Arabic and English. This is a thought that I discuss in detail in the conclusion, but for now I return to my teacher Ryan Goble who 'made connections where none seem possible or exist', an ability I consider an ancient art form that we find in the great epics. Unfortunately, humanity has forgotten this craft in our modern hyper-specialized world.

I make the intention that this book be approached as art, and I would like you to join me in engaging with it as such. In turn, please know that this book is definitively NOT an academic work. It is for this reason that I have omitted any footnotes or list of references, despite the abundance of quotations and cited sources. My reasoning is simple: I want to help my audience, as much as possible, <u>read</u> this work as they would a painting at a museum, suspending the rational faculty and instead <u>reeding</u> with hearts and emotions.

This strategy not only allows me to speak freely using ink, but also dissolves you of the anxiety to read footnotes, indices or references, as well as grants me the ability to convey meanings in silence, using some innovative approaches in writing. I am referring to two specific techniques I use throughout the proceeding chapters. The purpose of these performances is simple: to help us read between the lines, in emptiness beyond the grammar or content and more towards spirit and context.

The first is my inclusion of a quote on every page of chapters one through nine, excluding this preface and conclusion. These excerpts are by artists and sages in various crafts. I refer to these statements only rarely throughout the book; otherwise, they linger there in a deafening silence, for two purposes. First, in lieu of my conviction that the mystical experience is itself the creative process, I hope we all cherish the fact that every statement made by Ibn al-ʿArabi and other Sufi sages in this book has also been expressed, one way or another, by a non-Muslim artist.

The second reason for silently including these excerpts is to pay homage to a lesson in screenplay writing I learned from Ryan Goble: "Show don't tell!" This is my attempt to make this book an enjoyable guest to revisit time and again. I leave these empty spaces and awkward silence for you to have the time and space to <u>reflect</u> and <u>refract</u> while embraced by my words. I have weaved in my imagination distinct connections between these quotations and the words they breathe in me, but I am eager now to <u>perceive</u> and <u>receive</u> what they conjure in your heart.

The second performance in this book takes the form of underlined pairs of words that are either anagrams, homonyms, contranyms, or pairs that have some striking resemblance in my imagination. This is an homage to Ibn al-ʿArabi's own creative etymology that colors all of his writings. I need to make a disclaimer: my objective here is not simply to be witty, and definitely not to distract you from the content of the paragraphs. Rather, much like the quotations that stand alone, my purpose is to provide you with windows into your own imagination.

Ibn al-ʿArabi himself uses etymology as much more than a linguistic exercise but to encourage a metaphysical excursion, and this is my purpose as well. Some of these pairs reoccur often throughout the book, such as word and world, constriction and construction, or perceive and receive. Repetition is one of the most ancient strategies in birthing knowledge. As Sufi sages teach: "A sign of felicity in the ends is returning to the beginnings". Thus, I hope that every time you revisit one of these pairs, you see them in a new light and form.

Transitioning to other stylistic issues, many Muslim readers will know that the mentions of the prophet Muhammad ﷺ and God usually include some form of panegyric. I have decided to minimally include these. As you may have noticed, this Arabic sign ﷺ that translates to: "May God's blessings and prayers be upon him" is written after every mention of the prophet's name or title. This is the case almost always, notwithstanding instances where it was already mentioned and written in the same paragraph at least once.

As for God's name, I have decided to only capitalize pronouns that refer to Him and His direct names. Why do I include such panegyrical touches in an art book? Because they are ornaments that I believe can be appreciated by every artist. These are precisely the embellishments that transform the experience of reading a book from more than just a grammatical exercise to a performance that requires introspection, pause, even sometimes a dance.

I end this preface with a final word to my non-Muslim readers: this book is as much for you as – perhaps even more than – Muslim readers. Throughout the past few years, whenever I teach this topic, I regularly find non-Muslim artists to be the most receptive and comprehending of Ibn al-ʿArabi's metaphysics, especially pertaining to the spiritual dimensions of the creative process. Thus, I intentionally call the divine God, as opposed to Allah, because I am keenly aware and appreciate the divine wisdom in the 'cultural tongue'.

I imagine that the challenge for non-Muslim readers might actually be very similar to Muslims: learning an entirely new dimension of Islam that they had not been exposed to beforehand. Ibn al-ʿArabi is not a name that you will hear regularly in American mosques, unless you want to be accused of heresy and possibly excommunicated. And so, I write this book for the strangers on the margins.

I have created this space in ink for you and me, with the hope that Ibn al-ʿArabi can teach us how to be better creative spirits, while artists like Michael Caine and Al Pacino can inclucate in us universal lessons on how to be better human beings. I implore you, do not read my words as final, it would be a disservice to my own intention behind writing them. Rather, use them as a springboard for your own journey.

One of the central ideas you will find in the proceeding chapters is one coined by the French philosopher Jacques Derrida and his student John Caputo. In his book *On Religion*, Caputo states that "God is not the answer, but the opening of the question." This is how I always approach writing. Reading with the purpose of accumulating knowledge requires that each sentence and word has a definitive meaning. You will be gravely disappointed if you approach my book this way.

Instead, let us <u>read</u> each word as an opening of a question, and a fertile soil where we can <u>reed</u> our own flute. As I have learned, taught, and applied each of the connections that dance across these pages, I also hope that they will be of some benefit to you in your craft, and more importantly in helping you convey the intricacies of your creative process to other artists and larger society. Feel no hesitation to reach out to me about your thoughts and comments. <u>Reviews</u> are formal, but <u>purviews</u> are more personal.

For anybody who comes to this book with a vision of Islam as a dry legalistic tradition, or even worse a violent religion, I sincerely hope that this work changes your perspective. I do not care at all if this book encourages anyone to become Muslim. Rather, what I cherish most is that Islam, as a 'process of making meaning', emerges in your heart as a toolset that you can use in your craft, regardless of your faith or lack thereof. I want us to be Islam-ing artists as opposed to just Muslim ones.

Lastly, I would like to thank my dear friend, brother, and mentor prof. Rudolph Ware for being a companion on this road since 2012. I have been blessed to have you as a member of my dissertation committee, to receive your words as an introduction to this book, and most importantly for our countless conversations over Touba coffee, Jamaican jerk chicken, and fried plantains. From Michigan to Senegal, I am honored to call you brother.

Following the Traces: On Storytelling

"Tell stories so that they might reflect"
– Holy Qur'an (7:176)

"The universe is made of stories, not atoms"
– Muriel Rukeyser, *The Speed of Darkness*

If there is one movement that defines the human spirit, it is perhaps storytelling. From the drawings of cavemen to superheroes and science fiction, our species is one of storytellers. We have never told tales to pass or waste moments, but to form time, specifically a sacred sense of temporality that places us in the vast expanse of space, in the grandest scheme of things.

In every instance where we have tried to situate ourselves in relationship to what we cannot absorb through our immediate senses, which we have described as the unseen, we have been surprised to learn that ultimately we were sought prior to seeking, <u>longed</u> for <u>long</u> before <u>longing</u>, and are narrated <u>worlds</u> as a precursor to our desire to read the <u>words</u> of existence.

The world's three monotheisms, Judaism, Christianity, and Islam came upon a world stage that had hosted many plays, both tragedies and comedies. In turn, these three sacred traditions have honored the theater, actors, plots, and directors whence their holy scriptures are inundated with their own <u>stories</u>: sacred histories that are creative allusions to <u>His</u> – the divine – <u>Story</u>.

"No story lives unless someone wants to listen. The stories we love best do live in us forever."
– J.K. Rowling

In the Qur'an, Islam's sacred scripture, the word used for stories, *qasas*, is rich in meaning. Most pertinent is the derivative *iqtisas al-athar*, to follow the traces. Storytelling in the Qur'an is hardly a passive 'spectator sport', but rather an active process to both internalize and externalize the full spectrum of the narrative, including content, context, character, and style towards an embodied performance in the being of the listener.

James Morris calls this process *tahqiq* (self-realization), a term that is rooted in a larger conversation in the Arabic language surrounding divinity. We find the name of God <u>*al-Haqq*</u> (The Real), as well as the homonym <u>*haqq*</u> which means the 'right due to someone or something'. There is also the derivative term *haqiqa* (truth) that captures the reality of affairs as they are. Hence, we find in the sacred *hadith* (statement) of the prophet Muhammad ﷺ the following teaching: "Give everything – or one – that has a *haqq* [right] upon you their *haqq*".

There is a creative tension between *qasas*, the *tahqiq* of *haqiqa* (self-realization of truth/reality), and the actual narrative style in the Qur'an. In Arabic, there is a distinction between *qisas* and *qasas*: whereas the former describes a purely fictional tale, the latter indicates a historically accurate incident. However, Qur'anic stories are hardly presented as linear historical accounts. The same story of a prophet or people is dispersed over multiple chapters, often with omitted details and different dialogues in repeated segments.

"Things keep overlapping and blur, your story is part of your sister's story is part of many other stories, and there in no telling where any of them may lead."
– Erin Morgenstern, *The Night Circus*

To understand this unique style, we have to look at another term that the Qur'an uses to describe stories: *'ibrah*, a word that means lesson or exhortation but is etymologically related to other terms. First, we find *'ibarah*, the 'expression' that pays homage to the medium in which the *'ibrah* is conveyed (i.e., a written or orally transmitted story), *'ubur* or crossing-over from the shore of words to the worlds that reside behind them, and *i'tibar* or the active 'taking heed' of an exhortation and going through the journey of *'ubur*.

The Muslim sage Ibn al-'Arabi eloquently describes this linguistic and cosmological relationship between *'ibrah*, *'ibarah* and *'ubur* in his book *The Meccan Openings*:

> I have opened for you the *i'tibar* (taking heed). It is the passage from the form which manifests in the physical domain to what is related in your essence, or at the Side of al-*Haqq* [the Real]: that which signifies God. This is the figurative meaning of *i'tibar*. It is like "You have *'abarta*

(crossed over) the valley when you traversed it."

He made this life a *'ibrah* [example], or bridge that is *yu'bar* [crossed]. This means that it should be *tu'abbar* [to be interpreted], just as dreams that human beings see, while sleeping, are interpreted.

Ibn al-'Arabi connects the various threads of our conversation by tethering stories to reality and opening the window for us to perceive and realize – *tahqiq* – that the tales we <u>mold</u> are mirrors of our lives. They are made from the same <u>mold</u>, experiences, and memories.

> *"There is no greater agony than bearing an untold story inside you."*
> – Maya Angelou, *I Know Why the Caged Bird Sings*

Like Ibn al-'Arabi, William Shakespeare, a master of his own craft, had <u>riddled</u> his plays with this <u>riddle</u> of human existence. For example, in *As You Like It*, the character Jacques says: "And all the men and women merely players; They have their exits and their entrances, And one man in his time plays many parts." Likewise, in a memorable monologue in *The Tempest*, Prospero states:

> Our revels now are ended. These our actors,
> As I foretold you, were all spirits and
> Are melted into air, into thin air:
> And, like the baseless fabric of this vision,
> The cloud-capp'd towers, the gorgeous palaces,
> The solemn temples, the great globe itself,
> Ye all which it inherits, shall dissolve
> And, like this insubstantial pageant faded,
> Leave not a rack behind. We are such stuff
> As dreams are made on, and our little life
> Is rounded with a sleep.

In *Crossing and Dwelling*, Thomas Tweed tells us that: "Women and men make meaning and negotiate power as they appeal to contested historical traditions of storytelling, object making and ritual performance to make homes (dwellings) and cross boundaries (crossing/ *ʿubur*). Religions, in other words, involve finding one's place and moving through space."

What Ibn al-ʿArabi also gives us is a mimesis between <u>word</u> and <u>world</u>: the language of the story can – and should – perform the journey of *ʿubur* that both artist and audience undertake. The Muslim mystic, for whom Arabic was the language of the Sacred par excellence, would hardly perceive the closeness between even these two English terms: <u>word/world</u> as coincidental.

> *"The limits of my language mean the limits of my world."*
> – Ludwig Wittgenstein, *Tractatus logigo-philosphicus*

In the pre-modern understanding of language, to which Ibn al-ʿArabi adhered, the relationship between words and the meanings they signify is hardly haphazard. Rather, etymological roots and relationships allude to a metaphysical correspondence in the *unseen*, such as that between <u>word/world</u>. Let us take another example in Arabic pertaining to our conversation, which the Muslim mystic outlines.

The Arabic term for soul, *nafs*, belongs to the same family of the following words: *nafas* (breath), *nafis* (precious) and *tanfis* (alleviation). Building on this foundation, Ibn al-ʿArabi explains that our *nafas* is like a ship that carries the *nafis* meanings that reside in our *nafs*, all of which is a process of *tanfis*, alleviating the intense pressure of creative inspiration that resides in our souls. This does not end here, for Ibn al-ʿArabi needs to root the entire process of human creativity in its divine counterpart, since that is – for him – the ultimate source and origin for all cosmic movements and life.

There is an ongoing incessant mirroring between divinity (metacosm), the universe(s) (macrocosm) and human being (microcosm). This principle can be found in another teaching by the prophet Muhammad ﷺ: "The sickness is within you, and the cure is within you. You assume yourself to be something small, while within you is enfolded the entire universe."

And so, Ibn al-ʿArabi establishes this divine root for human creativity by conceiving God's Breath, *nafas al-rahman* as the *rahim* (womb) that surrounds the cosmos, in turn emphasizing that God's *rahma* (mercy) encompasses all of creation, an image that is mentioned explicitly in the Qur'an: "My Mercy has encompassed everything" (7:156).

> *"Our world is made up of a myriad of microcosms, of tiny worlds, each with its own habitues, everyone known to the others."*
> – Louis L'Amour, *Education of a Wondering Man*

Another set of linguistic relationships, pertaining to the image of Christ, reveals the extent to which Ibn al-ʿArabi takes this word/world mirroring to heart. *ʿIsa b. Maryam* (Jesus the son of Mary) who is described in the Qur'an as "The messenger of God, His Word and Spirit that He cast to Mary" (4:171) is the perfect channel to explore the possibility of a spiritual crucifixion that is embodied and performed in the very person of Christ.

The term for word in Arabic, *kalima*, is related to *kalim* (wound). In turn, Ibn al-ʿArabi perceives the entire cosmos as an empty canvas. Thenceforth, God's Words that are the created things arrive like various dyes that imprint themselves upon this plane and wound it. If every created thing is a word, then each part of us (e.g., physical, mental, spiritual) is a letter, whereas each stage in our life is a paragraph. Every community is a chapter that together comprise the tome of the human race.

The Qur'an comes to confirm this symbolism in the following verse: "On the day We fold the heavens and earth like the folding of a book. As We have begun the first creation, so do we return it. Indeed, this is a promise that We will fulfill" (21:104). Just as God has spoken this entire creation into being, as a divine epic, so do human beings involuntarily imitate this process through storytelling, art and what we regard as artisanship or creativity in various disciplines.

"Books help us understand who we are and how we are to behave. They show us what community and friendship mean; they show us how to live and die."
– Anne Lamott, *Bird by Bird*

When I was first exposed to this vision of our universe as a uni-verse in a larger macrocosmic ode, I began to wonder whether we are words in a poem or a lawbook written in prose? In other words – no pun intended – does God utter poetry or prose? Certainly, our existence is one of physical laws such as gravity and energy that hints to the fact that we may be a part of a prosaic lawbook.

The answer to my question came from Hazrat Inayat Khan, a celebrated 20th century Indian Muslim sitar musician, mystic and the founder of a large *tariqa* (Sufi path) in the West known as the Inayatiyya. In his book, *The Mysticism of Sound and Music*, the author confirms our poetic existence by emphasizing that everything that moves in this universe, ourselves included, follows a particular rhythm, much as can be found in a poem or song.

Khan is paying homage to the verse: "Indeed, in the creation of the heavens and earth and alternation of night and day are signs for those with [spiritual] centers" (3:190). In every cosmic movement there is a coordinated and divinely choreographed dance. Night and day keep switching roles on the heavenly stage, and their <u>play</u> is but an engine in the larger <u>prayer</u> of seasons.

This cycle of the four weather temperaments, part of our macrocosmic physical world, is also an homage to the circle of human life (microcosm). If we consider <u>Spring</u> to be the season when life <u>springs</u> into action, then the heat of summer is when our strength is at its peak, followed by old age and the wrinkled leaves of Autumn, when death comes, and greenery <u>falls</u> humbly towards entombment. Winter is then but a solemn burial procession, when the dead are covered in a shroud of gentle whiteness, awaiting the coming rebirth.

"Life is about rhythm. We vibrate, our hearts are pumping blood, we are a rhythm machine, that's what we are."
– Mickey Hart

As expected, this imagery is also mentioned and affirmed by the Qur'an: "And give the example of this life as water that We have brought down from heavens, whence it mingles with the plants of the earth, then becomes like dust, blown by the wind" (18:45). To return to the <u>word/world</u> mimesis, as each sentence in our lives is read, bringing us closer to the end of a chapter in our existence, so do the physical words also perish like leaves, leaving behind only solitary metaphors and allusions (e.g., <u>Fall</u>, <u>leaves/leaving</u>) that linger as nothing but memories of a lost remembrance.

And here we find ourselves in the presence of metaphors. As Ibn al-ʿArabi advised us above: life needs to be *tuʿabbar* (interpreted) like stories and dreams, because there is always more than meets the <u>I/eye</u>. This is a topic that the Muslim mystic explores with such creative rigor. Beginning with a dream of the prophet Muhammad ﷺ where he was given the choice to drink from three cups, one containing water, the other milk and last wine; he chose the middle. When asked for the meaning, he said: "I interpret it as taking the path of knowledge."

> *"If we shadows have offended,*
> *Think but this, and all is mended,*
> *That you have but slumbered here*
> *While these visions did appear.*
> *And this weak and idle theme,*
> *No more yielding but a dream,"*
> – William Shakespeare, *A Midsummer Night's Dream*

This ethereal symbolism materializes on the physical plane when the prophet ﷺ also instructs his community to offer the following formula of gratitude after eating food: "Oh God, bless us with what You have sustained us and grant us better than it", except when consuming milk, in which case one should say: "And increase us of it." Co-incidentally, this is also the formula prescribed in the Qur'an for seeking knowledge: "And say: 'My Lord, increase me in knowledge'" (20:114). And so, if drinking milk in a dream is a metaphor for receiving knowledge, the same can be said when we drink it in a waking state.

The importance of this uni-versal vision of our physical existence, dreams, and all that is in-between, is not only that it brings our slumbering visions closer to the material plane, but more importantly is the reverse movement of elevating and enchanting our physical messiness into the realm of the Sacred. Of course, as Thomas Tweed informed us, this is already what we human beings do, namely making meaning by 'crossing boundaries.' Nevertheless, we still need to decipher what this correspondence between <u>dreams</u> and the <u>reams</u> of our physical lives all <u>means</u> as pertains to the importance of the material metaphors in our daily existence.

In *God and Mystery of Words*, David Brown talks about this ancient understanding of the metaphor as more than a simple analogy, but an actual body that envelops the intended meaning. Metaphors are not meant to be left behind but embraced as they hold our hands while we step into the depths of meanings they signify. Much like the subtle pure spirit needs a dense body to manifest and appear in this physical world.

> *"Metaphors are much more tenacious than facts."*
> – Paul De Man

The same can be said about spiritual traditions, including Islam, Christianity, Judaism, Buddhism, or any other way of life that aims to provide depth and meaning to our existence. They also need to be embodied and made relevant through our stories; those that we live, write, or perform. It is through the messiness of our physical existence and paradoxical encounter with the Sacred in our imagination that hope is born.

Brown and Ibn al-ʿArabi both agree about this power of the metaphor as pertaining to the *logos*, which for Brown is the nature of Christ while for the Muslim mystic is *al-haqiqa al-muhammadiyya* (The Muhammadan Reality) or *al-nur al-muhammadi* (The Muhammadan Light), a concept for which we allocate an entire chapter in this book.

However, it is Ibn al-'Arabi specifically who creatively shows how the person of Christ is a perfect embodiment of the metaphor and its importance in our material existence. In his second most important book, *The Bezels of Wisdom*, the author dedicates an entire chapter to the person of Jesus, beginning by focusing not only on his immaculate conception or virgin birth, but also the importance of his physical form.

"Every religion is true one way or another. It is true when understood metaphorically."
– Joseph Campbell, *The Power of Myth*

The Muslim mystic begins with verses of poetry that position Jesus as a *barzakh* (isthmus) between the physical and spiritual realms:

> From the water of Mary or the breath of Gabriel,
> In the form of a mortal fashioned of clay,
> Because of this, his sojourn was prolonged,
> Enduring, by decree, more than a thousand years.
> A spirit from none other than God,
> So that he might raise the dead and bring forth birds from clay.
> God purified him in body and made him transcendent
> In the Spirit, making him like Himself in creating.

The miracle of Christ is more than the absence of a biological father, but also the way in which his body, despite being identical to that of other human beings outwardly, actually affected and directed his spiritual dimension and extraordinary feats of power.

First, Ibn al-'Arabi tells us that Jesus continues to live for more than a thousand years since his birth – a foundational belief in Islam – not necessarily because of his spirit but rather body that allows him to linger in the material realm. In the last verse, the Muslim mystic also emphasizes that Jesus' body was purified and made transcendent in spirit', whence he was able to <u>create</u> like God, an homage to <u>divine creativity</u>.

And yet, this artistic ability granted to Jesus is not independent of his physical form, but rather intimately tethered to it. Ibn al-ʿArabi tells us that Jesus was only able to perform the miracles mentioned in the Qur'an, such as resurrecting the dead, curing the blind and lepers and breathing life into a bird formed of clay, while in human form "because that is the image that the holy spirit Gabriel appeared when he breathed the Word of God, that is Jesus, into his mother Mary."

> *"Art is a reflection of God's creativity, evidence that we are made in the image of God."*
> – Francis Schaeffer

The Muslim mystic does not halt there but goes even further by emphasizing that when Gabriel appeared to Mary in the form of a handsome man, she had secluded herself from her people and was frightened because she thought he wanted to harm her. Thus, Gabriel had to assure Mary that he is a messenger from God and wait for her to become tranquil, because "had he breathed the Word of God into her in that condition, Jesus would have been born in a frightening form such that no one could look at him."

This power of Christ's physical form even extends to his community which is characterized by impeccable humility, as the Qur'an mentions: "You will find the closest people to the believers those who say we are Christian, that is because among them are priests and monks who are not arrogant" (5:82).

This humility, the Muslim mystic states, is due to the humbleness that Jesus inherited from his mother Mary.

Jesus for Ibn al-'Arabi is not only a historical figure, but like all prophets and sages is an archetype and performance of a sacred principle, in this case divine creativity. Every human being is born to physical parents while the affair of our spirit remains in the unseen. In the case of Christ, both the physical and spiritual dimensions unfolded on the material stage, with Mary representing the motherly body and Gabriel representing the fatherly spirit.

"Accept the seasons of your heart, even as you have always accepted the seasons that pass over your fields. And you would watch with serenity through the winters of your grief."
– Khalil Gibran, *The Prophet*

And so, just as God uttered the verse that is Jesus, in breath and <u>form</u>, Christ – in turn – reenacted his own miraculous birth throughout his preaching of the Gospel. He could only manifest this performance because it was an imprinted memory in his being. His <u>art</u> was a dance choreographed in his <u>heart</u>. This much we know from the familial relationships between *nafs* (soul), *nafas* (breath), *nafis* (precious) and *tanfis* (alleviation) that we discussed earlier.

If Christ is a performance of God's creative power, then we may go even further and say that divine creativity, and by mirroring, its human counterpart is a 'Christic' process. Even though God tells a story through everything He creates, Jesus is a particularly unique instance because he performs outwardly the divine creative process. The stories we tell are also breaths that pay homage to this unfolding journey and, thus, resemble divine art.

Moreover, if Christ is a divine poem, we must not forget the vessel, Mary who carried this inspiration from conception to birth. In the Qur'an, God describes the pure condition of Mary as the fertile soil in which the conception of Jesus was possible: "Mary the daughter of ʿImran who guarded her chastity, whence We breathed in her of Our Spirit, and she believed in the Words of her Lord and was among the pious" (66:12).

Like Mary, every storyteller is a single parent who receives the breath of inspiration, carries it to maturity, then births it into a work of art. But how does the scriptural description of Mary above apply to the rest of human beings as storytellers? What does it mean to guard one's chastity, believe in the Words of the Lord and be among the pious for all of humanity as storytellers, believers and non-believers alike?

> *"God made man because he loves stories."*
> – Elie Wiesel, *The Gates of the Forest*

Our faculties, including the five senses, imagination, and memory are the <u>womb</u> wherein the seed of creative inspiration is first <u>entombed</u> then resurrected into a living work of art, much like Mary's womb carried and conceived Jesus. In turn, guarding the chastity of our creative womb ought to mean that we do not commit 'creative adultery', allowing anything other than the sacred Word of God into our senses, because all of that will ultimately shape the stories we tell.

However, such a narrow understanding of 'creative chastity' neither bodes well with the richness of this Qur'anic verse nor allows for a more genuine engagement with art and creativity in our present day and age, where many artists and storytellers are either non-believers, in the religious sense, or for whom religion plays no part in their craft.

I hold that 'creative chastity' must be understood alongside the second description of Mary in this verse, that she 'believed in the Words of her Lord,' and what are these <u>Words</u> except the <u>World</u> as uni-verse(s)? How can we only carry the Sacred in our 'creative womb' while at the same time embrace all that is around us, the good and ugly? Precisely by perceiving all as an enchanted Word, a divine gift in the <u>form</u> of a prompt to help us <u>form</u> the contours of our story.

> *"The position of the artist if humble. He is essentially a channel."*
> – Piet Mondrian

Ibn al-ʿArabi's perception of Jesus seeks to <u>construct</u>, not <u>constrict</u>, our own Christic process known as creativity. The metaphor in Jesus, his physical body, exercises visible power in his meaning as a Word of God, his spirit. What remains to be excavated from this vision is the importance of memory in <u>forging</u> a story that is authentic, not <u>forged</u>. How can we open ourselves to the infinite procession of external manifestations while listening to the soliloquy within?

As we have seen, Jesus is only able to tell a story that pays homage to his own birth. His artwork was a repeated return to a perplexing miracle, of heaven meeting earth and spirit marrying body in the material realm. There is a similar imprint in every human being that will guide and color the stories they tell. It is a constant dance between being <u>silent</u> in order to <u>listen</u> for the Words with-out that seek to remind us of the Worlds with-in.

This is a calling for authenticity at the deepest level, which requires two wings of inner and outer taste. The *nafis* (precious) meanings that reside in our *nafs* (soul), carried by *nafas* (breath), cannot be found in anybody else. Ibn al-ʿArabi is emphatic about this maxim: "There is no repetition in creation." He also quotes a celebrated 10th century predecessor, Junayd al-Baghdadi who replied when asked about *maʿrifa* (inner gnosis of the heart): "The color of water is that of the cup."

> *"Memory is a great artist. For every man and for every woman it makes the recollection of his or her life a work of art and an unfaithful record."*
> – Andre Maurois

Our souls are like these vessels, each with a different shape and color and embellished by memories that make us sacred miracle-performers through storytelling. The shape and color in which I perceive the world, shaped by my own memories and experiences is necessarily different than every other human being's cup, even those closest to me. However, although my vessel is unique, it is also limited hence my need to learn and embrace stories forged by others; not to replicate, but to better understand my own narrative.

Perhaps you feel that your memories are stained by the profane; if so, then how can they be a breath in your story? Whose life has not been mired by darkness. Can light even be light save when facing the density of nothingness? We are all paradoxical meetings between heaven and earth, purity and filth, piety and sin. That eccentricity and paradox is precisely what grants us human beings our biggest miracle: storytelling.

The tale of another prophet in the Qurʾan highlights the importance of our past and memories in guiding and sustaining the direction we take in life. The tale of Moses is the perfect example of the Qur'an's unique storytelling style. It is dispersed over many chapters and follows a non-linear chronology where we first meet Moses as an adult leading the Israelites away from Egypt to the promised land.

Later, in chapter 20 titled *Taha*, we are introduced to his birth, at a time when Pharaoh sought to kill all the Israelites' first-born males. His mother places her newly born infant in a basket in the Nile that then reaches Pharaoh's palace. The latter's heart softens for the infant and raises him to be his very undoing. Moses' extraordinary physical strength leads him to inadvertently kill an Egyptian man; and so, he becomes a fugitive. After marrying one of the daughters of Shuʿayb, another prophet who lived in nearby Madyan, Moses leads his family through the wilderness where he meets God, for the first time, at the burning bush.

> *"As a man you should know who is right and who is wrong. You must make decisions and enforce them. As a writer you should not judge. You should understand."*
> – Ernest Hemingway, *On Writing*

I want us to keep in mind that Moses is a fugitive who killed another human being. When God speaks to him, He immediately informs Moses that he is to be ordained a messenger to Pharaoh; the same ruler who is seeking justice against him for murder. This newly designated prophet of God is to preach morality to one of the worst dictators of his time.

In other chapters of the Qur'an, Moses exclaims why he is unworthy to be a prophet, especially to Pharaoh and his people: "I have killed someone from them, and I am afraid they will kill me" (28:33). God's response to his prophet's fear in chapter 20 is utterly breathtaking:

> We have bestowed Our Bounty upon you another time. When We revealed to your mother what was revealed: "Put him in the tomb [basket] then in the river. Let it deliver him to the shore whence an enemy of mine and his will take him.
>
> **And I bestowed upon you a love from Me, so that you are molded under My Gaze**, whence your sister walks among them: "Can I tell you about someone who will take care of him?" Like so, We returned you to your mother so that her eye may become tranquil and not sad.
>
> *Then you killed a soul*, so We saved you from that misery and tested you into maturity. Then you remained for a few years among the people of Madyan, until you have come here according to a measured degree, oh Moses. Indeed, **I have molded you for my sake.**

Between the two bolded statements expressing deep divine love there emerges the mention of murder. And yet, that act was but one of many measured steps that had delivered Moses to God, wherefrom he will be sent back to Pharaoh as a prophet.

"Perhaps things are most beautiful when they are not quite real; when you look upon a scene as an outsider, and come to possess it in its entirety and forever; when you live in the present with the lucidity and feeling of memory; when, for want of connection, the world deepens and becomes art."
– Mark Helprin

There are many lessons to be gleaned from this paradoxical encounter between Moses and God. First, like Mary who was a single parent and carrier of the creative inspiration that would become Jesus, the mother of Moses had also given birth to a story waiting to unfold, unfortunately at a time when these specific stories were killed at every turn; their letters ripped before they had the opportunity to ripen.

As a carrier, channel, and deliverer of her son, she was tested with a universal rite that every storyteller and artist must go through: after birthing your work, you are made to place it in the <u>tomb</u> of 'letting-go', with complete conviction that it will <u>find</u> its way to salvation, where it will be <u>founded</u> as a <u>tome</u>, <u>memory</u> and <u>remembrance</u>. Incidentally, the mother of the prophet Muhammad ﷺ had uttered these final words to her son moments before her death, when he was just 7 years old: "My son, I have conceived you in purity, gave birth to you in purity, and you shall remain after me a memory/remembrance!"

As we continue our journey to the next section, where we explore a Sufi cosmology of the creative process, we end this chapter with a solemn appreciation of each moment in our lives, the beautiful and ugly, good and evil, dense and subtle. They come together like clashing waves of red and blue in a beautiful dance on the canvas of our unique identities. It is through storytelling that <u>memories</u> of dark <u>moments</u> in our lives can heal. Are they embellished? Yes! Are they factual? Hardly! But is it at least art? Absolutely, and that is all that matters.

52

The Hidden Treasure: On the Creative Process

"Do you have the courage to bring forth the treasures that are hidden within you?"
– Elizabeth Gilbert, Big Magic

I like to think of *awliya'* (Sufi saints/sages) as artists of the soul, and artists – regardless of religious affiliation – as saints in soul and heart. As I mentioned in the preface, art for me is best described as a translation process of what is ineffable into the tangible and making connections where none seem possible or exist. Like artists, who destabilize and question the <u>constricted</u> perceptions of their age, in order to <u>construct</u> new visions and engagements with reality, Sufi saints have often been accused by their co-religionists of *kufr* (disbelief/heresy) and *shatahat* (blameworthy utterances).

And yet, like Edgar Allen Poe or Vincent Van Gogh whose works were appreciated only after their passing, saints like Ibn al-'Arabi were – and still are – opposed by those who refuse to venture into what the Sufi poet Rumi describes as "the field beyond belief and un-belief". Mark Hederman, an abbot from Ireland, states unabashedly that modern societies usually pay no attention to artists and the visions they communicate or channel, until after their death.

One of my spiritual guides, Shaykh Hisham Kabbani, had proclaimed a similar sentiment when I informed him about a speaking engagement that I had once at an event exploring spirituality and art. He said: "Art is all spirituality and spirituality is all art. You need good *dhawq* [taste] to appreciate art as well as follow a spiritual path." He had also hinted towards Ibn al-ʿArabi's status as an 'artist of the soul' by stating that "not everybody with knowledge of Arabic can understand him, only a poet."

> *"Art is born and takes hold wherever there is a timeless and insatiable longing for the spiritual"*
> – Andrei Tarkovsky

If we consider art in the second sense, as making connections where none seem possible or exist, then saints are definitely artists. They regularly quote *athar* (statements/expressions) that many legalistic Muslim scholars deem inauthentic and dubious. Perhaps the best example of such an *athar* is that pertaining to the 'hidden treasure', the focus of this chapter. Ibn al-ʿArabi, like other Muslim saints, relies on this teaching extensively and knows all too well of the legal scholars' mistrust in its authenticity.

And yet, as a divinely ordained 'artist of the soul', he exclaims unequivocally that "despite its inauthenticity according to the science of *hadith*, it is authenticated by the people of God [saints] according to *kashf* [unveiling].” Ibn al-ʿArabi regards *kashf* as the highest form of intellection, definitively loftier than rational reflection. Whereas the *ʿaql* (rational faculty) is limited to the physical domain, affairs of the spiritual world demand the flexible fluctuations of the *qalb* (heart), so that it can dance across the waves of cosmic movements.

The Muslim mystic retorts here to his creative etymology, tethering *ʿaql* to the derivative term *ʿiqal* (leash) and *qalb* to *taqallub* (fluctuation) as well as its adverbial homonym *qalb* (overturning). As we ascend in our perception and experience of cosmic reality, we also learn to let go of rational constriction, instead embracing heart-based construction. As well will see, this is not only pertaining to *suluk* (self-discipline), but the journey of art and creativity as well.

> *“If I create from the heart, nearly everything works; if from the head, almost nothing.”*
> – Mark Chagall

This is also the spirit moving through the *athar* of the hidden treasure, wherein God says: “I was a Hidden Treasure, and I loved to be known. Thus, I created creation that I may be known by them.” Ibn al-ʿArabi explains that this statement was God’s response to David when he asked about the purpose of creation. At this peak of mysticism, a universal truth emerges across many spiritual traditions: “For so God loved the world” and “I loved to be known”.

Underlying the vastness of this poetic purpose of creation is a sophisticated ontological framework that outlines Ibn al-ʿArabi’s cosmogenesis, or vision of the beginning of the universe. This concept, known as *maratib al-wujud* (the levels of being) is a good starting point towards a better understanding of the creative process through the lens of Sufism. From metaphysics, through love and finally reaching art, one can appreciate the wholesome unitary vision of an 'artist of the soul' like Ibn al-ʿArabi.

Although the Muslim mystic himself did not outline these levels of being, a later figure in his school, Saʿid al-Din Farghani provided the paradigm while writing a commentary on the celebrated *Khamriya* (Wine Ode) of ʿUmar b. al-Farid. Although other sages in the school of Ibn al-ʿArabi had provided a similar outline, Farghani's is most harmonious with our journey due to his emphasis on the human subject (microcosm) as a synthesis of the uni-verse(s) (macrocosm).

"Poetry and painting are done in the same way you make love; it's an exchange of blood, a total embrace – without caution, without any thought of protecting yourself."
– Joan Miro

Beginning at the pinnacle of being, there is the *hadra* (presence) of *lahut* (divinity), this is a reference to the divine Essence prior to any creative motive, otherwise known as *ahadiyya* (absolute singularity). After this comes the presence of *malakut* (kingdom), where the intelligibles reside, including spiritual beings that manifest God's names and attributes. It is this presence that human beings usually refer to as the *ghayb* (unseen).

The third is that of *jabarut* (dominion), which Ibn al-ʿArabi describes as *ʿalam al-khayal* (the realm of imagination) and most crucial aspect of ancient cosmology for art and creativity. We will discuss this level in more detail in chapter 4, "On Paradox and Imagination". The next presence is that of *nasut* (physical world), including the vast reaches of the cosmos that we can now perceive where the realities of all higher realms project themselves and embrace us in our three-dimensional existence.

The last presence, *al-insan al-kamil al-tamm* (the perfect and complete human) is the culmination and synthesis of all the higher realms. They all manifest, <u>reflect</u> and <u>refract</u> harmoniously in human body, mind, and spirit. If Nietzsche was worried that a fake 'Übermensch' is one who forsakes the mired and messy physical existence for the sake of a distant afterlife, he need not be afraid of *al-insan al-kamil al-tamm*, for that is one who hosts our eccentric and paradoxical bodily world in a meeting with an enchanted Sacred. In him or her, all these realities speak of everything: our <u>prayers </u>as well as the way we <u>play</u>; all of it matters.

> *"The <u>Übermensch</u> shall be the meaning of the earth! I entreat you my brethren, remain true to the earth, and do not believe those who speak to you of supra-terrestrial hopes! … Behold, I teach you the Übermensch. He is this lightning, he is this madness! … Behold, I am a prophet of the lightning and a heavy drop from the cloud: but this lightning is called Übermensch."*
> – Friedrich Nietzsche, *Thus Spoke Zarathustra*

We will also have recourse to speak again of this concept in the following chapter, "On Artist as Art". For now, let us visualize the five *maratib al-wujud* (levels of being) using the diagram on the following page. Returning to the *athar* of the hidden treasure, we can also perceive five stages of divine manifestations that correspond to these levels of being. First, "I was a hidden treasure" is the presence of *lahut* (divinity). As the prophet ﷺ himself described this first stage: "God was and nothing was with Him", or as he said elsewhere: "No one truly knows God except Him." Both expressions are apt descriptors of *lahut* as the hidden treasure.

Second, the presence of *malakut* (kingdom) corresponds to "I loved." This signals God's first movement, breath, and desire to manifest His names and attributes on the empty canvas of creation. Just as our *nafas* (breath) gives *tanfis* (alleviation) to our *nafs* (soul) by externalizing the *nafis* (precious) creative inspiration that resides in us, so does *nafas al-rahman* (breath of the most-merciful) also provide, as Ibn al-ʿArabi eloquently describes: "Alleviation from *al-karb al-ilahi* [divine pressure]", by manifesting the infinitude of creative potentiality hidden in the divine essence.

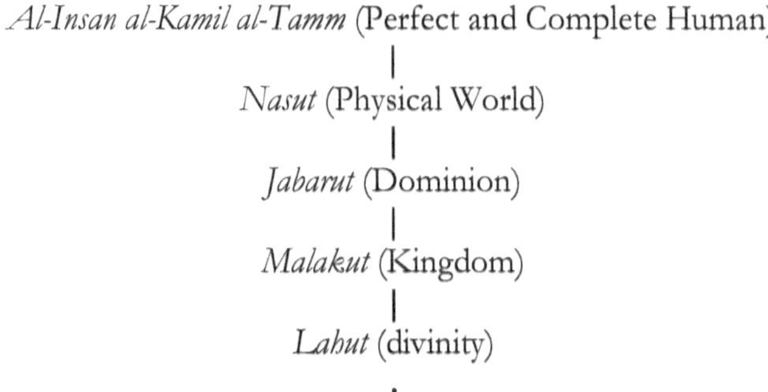

> *"Every picture shows a spot with which the artist has fallen in love."*
> – Alfred Sisley

And yet, as the prophet ﷺ also tells us in the second part of the teaching mentioned above: "And He is as He has always been." As uni-verse(s) continue to expand majestically, God's unknown essence remains, in absolute singularity, a hidden treasure. Ibn al-ʿArabi comments on this paradox by explaining that if one chooses to look at the expanse of creation from the vantage point of multiplicity, this they will find to no end. And if they so desire to find oneness, that they will also find to no end. The Muslim mystic describes this beautifully as: "I have come to a shore [creation] without an ocean [divinity] and an ocean without a shore."

Third, the presence of *jabarut* (dominion) aligns with "to be known." Here, the love and desire to externalize divine creativity manifests in the first order of created entities: pure intelligibles that are absolutely subtle and unbounded by time and space. They are so transparent in their <u>reflection</u> and <u>refraction</u> of the divine names and attributes that viewers are perplexed as to whether they are witnessing divinity itself or merely a mirror.

"I think some of the biggest bursts of creativity and artistic growth I've had are usually preceded by a big creative block."
– Ashley Goldberg

Fourth, we have the presence of *nasut* (physical world) that corresponds to "I created creation." This is the moment when the divine creative process not only manifests in spirit but also dresses itself in a bodily form. In turn, these divine works of art take on a life of their own in the fifth and final stage of *al-insan al-kamil al-tamm* (the perfect and complete human). This perfect mirror of divinity has will power and chooses to synthesize the levels of being in complete harmony, such that *lahut, malakut, jabarut* and *nasut* are present in a perfect equilibrium.

Incorporating these stages of the *athar* into the above diagram, we obtain the updated visual on the following page that provides a more intimate taste of the metaphysical outline of *maratib al-wujud*; one that voices God's love and desire in the first person. We now have the necessary foundation to envision a corresponding five stages of the creative process that begin, end, and return to the levels of being within the artist.

The consummate artists are those who are instances of *insan kamil tamm* in progress, synthesis of the macrocosmic uni-verse(s) and microcosmic creative potentiality. Just as "God is now as He has always been", a hidden treasure, so should a metaphysic of the creative process reveal to artists that they are in a constant flux between their inner creative potential and the birthed work that they conceive then carry to maturity.

What the primordial presence of *lahut* – the hidden treasure – <u>reveals</u> to us of the creative process is the <u>revelation</u> that 'creative block' is not a state of withholding, but an imminent flood. We <u>revel</u> in the ebb and flow of this sacred movement. Just as Ibn al-ʿArabi witnessed an endless shore return to its infinite home, the ocean, so does our creative inspiration also need to go back to the source from time to time, <u>abiding</u> in <u>hiding</u> before resurfacing with new riches from our hidden treasure.

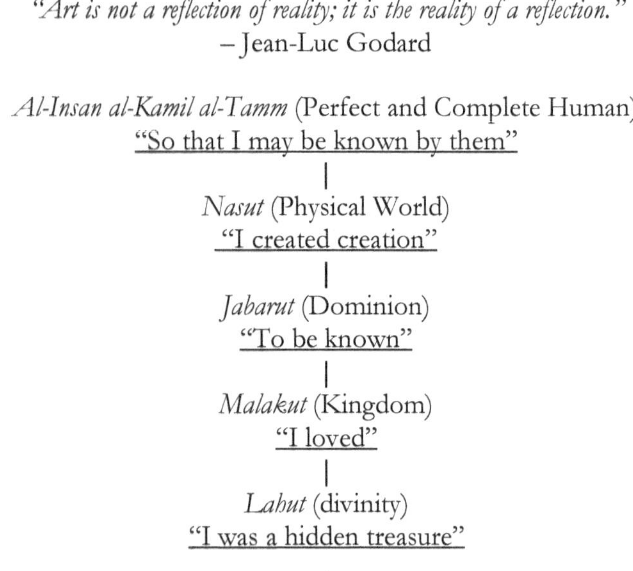

> *"Art is not a reflection of reality; it is the reality of a reflection."*
> – Jean-Luc Godard

When our creative inspiration is ready to awaken after a much-needed slumber, we feel it. We recognize its presence, even though it is a pure intelligible spirit with neither name nor form. The writer feels the story as a black hole of protagonist, antagonist, setting and climax. The painter touches all the colors on the spectrum at the tips of their brush, and the musician can feel every cadence and crescendo in their <u>piece</u> as a singular eternal utterance, what Hazrat Inayat Khan calls *sawt sarmad* (the primordial sound of <u>peace</u>). This is love at first <u>sight</u>, at the holiest of <u>sites</u>.

> *"You use a glass mirror to see your face. You use works of art to see your soul."*
> – George Bernard Shaw

The word for 'beloved' in Arabic conveys the transparency of this initial deluge of creativity. *Habib* is a term that means both lover and beloved. The purity of our inner hidden treasure's reflection in this infant creative inspiration initially <u>confounds</u> before <u>con-founding</u> us. We are uncertain whether it is just a mirror or the abyss of riches itself. As we meander around our perplexity and raise our inspiration to maturity, we realize there is no difference. Meanwhile, the mirror is incessant: "<u>be loved beloved</u>!"

Then, we begin to translate our creative inspiration into a work of art, "to be known", all the while feeding this intelligible infant with words, colors, sounds or whatever language our creative medium speaks. We see and <u>hear</u> it take shape <u>here</u> and now. We remember that "God was, and nothing was with Him, and He is now as He has always been." And so, we feel like Nietzsche's 'superman' and sense that this new work is an unfolding of everything we hold within, even though as a 'shore without an ocean' it is a mere drop from our ineffable hidden treasure.

When the work of art is finally born, from the womb of our inner *lahut*, we realize that we have undertaken our rite of "I created creation." The painting, poem, film, or song are breathing back to us our memories. We see our creative process performed with every contour, <u>fault</u>, and <u>fault-line</u> between artist and art. There is almost no separation at this point between "I created creation" and "so that I may be known by them." The work is already questioning us: crying, <u>smiling</u>, and drawing <u>similes</u> beyond our control.

> *"Creativity doesn't wait for that perfect moment. It fashions its own perfect moments out of ordinary ones."*
> – Bruce Garrabrandt

In this way, the metacosmic divine creative process, manifesting through the exhalation of life in the cosmos and the ensuing inhalation – otherwise known as the return journey to oneness – is intimately tethered to the macrocosmic galaxies and heavens, each of which is rotating around its own axis of inner creativity. All of this majesty brilliantly enters a single point of stillness in the microcosm known as the human being. Everything that we <u>witness</u> is enfolded within us, even that which we cannot perceive by our <u>wit</u>, of movements that overwhelm and force us to acknowledge our fragile existence.

In another well-known *hadith,* the prophet ﷺ teaches that God says: "Neither my heavens nor earth can encompass Me, but the heart of my believing servant can envelop Me." And if – as they say – 'imitation is the highest form of flattery', then what higher expression of love is there than to <u>reform</u> ourselves by dressing the meanings that reside in our souls with new <u>forms</u>: the truest sense of <u>reformation</u>.

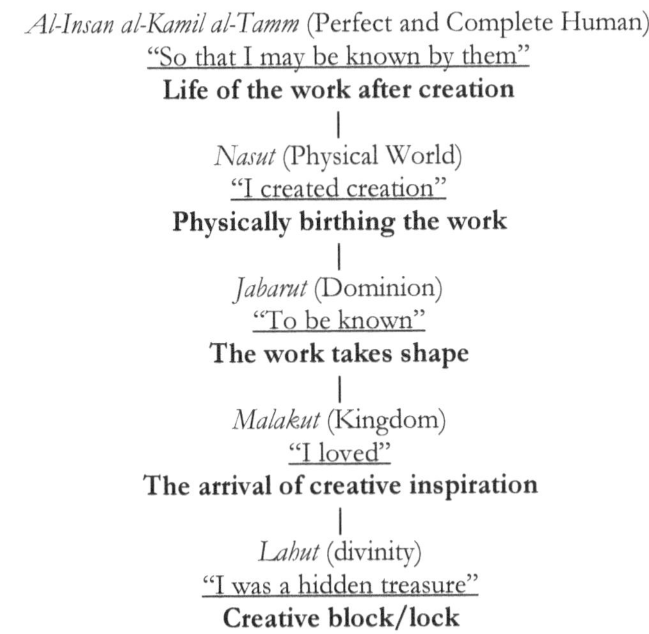

In *Big Magic*, Elizabeth Gilbert tells a wondrous experience where a story that was still in the infant stage of "I loved", in that inner presence of *malakut* departed <u>away</u> only to find <u>a way</u> into another writer's heart, Ann Patchett. However, once the external impetus for the tale, a fiction based on the Amazon in Brazil, had presented itself to Patchett, it became clothed in the latter's unique hidden treasure. Afterall, despite the affability between Gilbert and Patchett, theirs are two distinct vessels, each with a different shape and color in which the water of creativity may live and breathe.

Gilbert also converses with Ibn al-ʿArabi in a way that helps us better understand the five levels of being in the creative process, just as the Muslim mystic aids in appreciating the mercy in our hidden treasure and artistic *lahut* known as creative block. Describing the sudden ways in which creative inspiration visits the artist, after its slumber, the author of *Big Magic* mentions another writer, Ruth Stone and her exquisite account of a muse's visitation.

Stone states that "she could hear a poem coming toward her – hear it rushing across the landscape at her, like a galloping horse." In response, "she would 'run like hell' toward the house, trying to stay ahead of the poem, hoping to get to a piece of paper and pencil fast enough to catch it." When she does 'catch' the poem, "she would be able to grab it and take dictation." Otherwise, if the poem doesn't leave, in very rare instances "she would just barely catch it … 'by the tail'. Like grabbing a tiger. Then she would almost physically pull the poem back into her with one hand … the poem would appear on the page from the last word to the first – backward, but otherwise intact."

> *"Nature is a revelation of God; Art a revelation of man."*
> – Henry Wadsworth Longfellow

Our <u>prayer</u> of creativity is ultimately a <u>play</u> between our inner universe and outer cosmos. These two books are known by Muslim sages as *al-kitab al-marqum* (the cryptic book) and *al-kitab al-manzur* (witnessed book), respectively. The third tome, scripture, is described as *al-kitab al-mastur* (the lined book). These three sources of knowledge mirror one another perfectly and completely. Not a thing that is <u>founded</u> or withers in one of them save that it can be <u>found</u> in the other.

Most often, the exquisite and enchanted Sacred will never speak to us as creative inspiration through the <u>unfamiliar</u>. On the contrary, it always chooses the deeply close, the almost <u>familial</u>. However, this happens in unforeseen ways, in paths and images that <u>sunder</u> any intimacy with our world like <u>thunder</u>. Art is not about <u>words</u> that are difficult to <u>understand</u>, rather those that we have always <u>stood under</u>, yet now create new <u>worlds</u> for us that we never <u>expected</u>: they channel the <u>exceptional</u>.

The French anthropologist Claude Lévi-Strauss speaks of *bricolage* as the process of making something new from a known and limited set of tools. This is precisely the brilliance of the artist as a *bricoleur* who works with what they and others around them have already perceived and understood in a specific way. However, they upend these habits and overthrow their governance. Then, they keep <u>turning</u> them until all <u>returns</u> a miracle.

"Art makes the familiar strange so that it can be freshly perceived. To do this it presents its material in unexpected, even outlandish ways: the shock of the new."
– Viktor Shklovsky

Ruth Stone perceives her creative inspiration in a form that is familiar to her surroundings in rural Virginia: a galloping horse. Gilbert received the spirit for her initial story about the Amazon from her partner who comes from Brazil. I will often receive my divine gift, a daily poem, in the form of a smell, texture or phonetic breath from my motherland(s): Iraq and Egypt. Sometimes it might even be a subtle whisper from the spirit of one of my muses from that region, such as Nizar Kabbani, Naguib Mahfouz or Mahmoud Darwish.

In his interview on *Inside the Actor's Studio* with the late James Lipton, Steven Spielberg discussed the inspiration for his film *Close Encounters of the Third Kind.* The director mentioned that he had always been fascinated with what resides in space and fearful of what lives deep under the ocean. Hence, he made films like *E.T.* and *Jaws*, respectively. And yet, he had been unaware of just how much the familial in life had clothed these passions on screen.

It was not until Lipton asked Spielberg whether the inspiration for the final scene in *Close Encounters* – where aliens communicate with human beings via music that is played on a computer screen – was an homage to the director's parents, one of whom was a musician and the other a computer scientist. Spielberg replied, with an emotional and tearful smile: "Not until this moment did I realize that this was supposed to be my mother and father. Thank you for that."

"They always say time changes things, but you actually have to change them yourself."
– Andy Warhol

Ultimately, all human beings are *bricoleurs*. As Tweed tells us in the first chapter: "Women and men make meaning and negotiate power as they appeal to contested historical traditions of storytelling, object making and ritual performance to make homes (dwelling) and cross boundaries (crossing/ *ʿubur*)." We take objects, artifacts, and images that are <u>near</u> and <u>dear</u> to us, then weave them in such a way that they may take us afar.

And I believe this is a central motif animating our journey in this chapter on the metaphysics of the creative process: we need the <u>familiar/familial</u> to remain sane and calm on our journey into the unknown. In her mystical commentary on the prophet Muhammad's ﷺ *sira* (biography), the 20th century lady saint Amina ʿAdil recounts an extraordinary story from the prophet's celebrated *miʿraj* (ascension) journey.

After passing through the seven heavens and boundaries of the cosmos, beyond which no creation had ever ventured, the prophet ﷺ reaches a place of incredible *wahsha* (loneliness). There was nothing, a true manifestation of "God was, and nothing was with Him, and He is now as He has always been." Suddenly, he hears the voice of his closest companion Abu Bakr. He felt both tranquil and surprised to hear his friend's voice, so far away from the material realm. It was only after this incident that he was admitted into the divine presence where God spoke to him.

"An artist is always alone - if he is an artist. No, what the artist needs is loneliness."
– Henry Miller

The prophet ﷺ asked God whether Abu Bakr had been gifted this auspicious journey before him, since he heard his voice moments prior. God's response reminisces of His loving conversations with two other prophets. He states that when Moses came to speak with Him at the burning bush, he also felt a *wahsha*, due to the overwhelming encounter. And so, in order to alleviate [*tanfis*] the anxiety that Moses felt, God asked him: "What is that in your right hand, Moses?" (20:17)

The prophet of the Israelites replied: "It is my staff, upon which I lean, guide my sheep, and for which I have other needs." At that extraordinary moment, when Moses was reminded of what was familiar to him, tranquility returned. Similarly, God tells the prophet ﷺ that He had created an angel with the form and voice of Abu Bakr to relieve him of his loneliness. He also tells him that just as Moses leaned upon his cane, so is Abu Bakr his figurative staff. The prophet of Islam will lean on him in his hardest tribulations.

In this instance, we are also reminded of Mary and her fright when visited by the holy spirit who would breathe and cast the word of Jesus into her womb. As Ibn al-ʿArabi informed us, had Gabriel cast the spirit of Christ into Mary at that moment of fear, his physical image would correspond to the condition of his mother, whence no one could bare looking at him. He also showed us how our physicality guides and ornaments our spirituality; they <u>shape</u> the stories we tell and <u>mold</u> our creative process.

"A master in the art of living draws no sharp distinction between his work and his play; his labor and his leisure; his mind and his body; his education and his recreation. He hardly knows which is which."
– François-René de Chateaubriand

There is also an extraordinary harmony between Mary's meeting with Gabriel and the prophet's ﷺ own encounter with this angel who – according to Islamic creed – was tasked with delivering the divine revelation known as the Qurʾan to the prophet of Islam. However, there is another meeting that highly reminisces of Mary's encounter with the holy spirit. This incident is particularly significant because it was witnessed by all the prophet's companions.

Just as he had appeared to Mary, Gabriel entered a gathering of the prophet ﷺ in the form of a handsome young man. He sat across and asked him a series of questions, one of which was: "Tell me about *ihsan* [perfective beauty]?" To this the prophet replied: "It is that you worship God as though you see Him. For indeed, if you do not perceive Him, then [know that] He perceives you." For Muslim sages, the word *ihsan* [perfective beauty] is another term for Sufism, the ocean of Islamic mysticism in which we are sailing in this book.

And so, Sufism is ultimately about 'worshipping God' – an overarching notion that covers all our engagements with the unseen, including our hidden treasure – 'as though we see Him.' Commenting on this incident, Ibn al-ʿArabi states that the prophetic response: 'as though you see Him' is a command to imagine God, in form, during prayer. We ought to clothe Him with those images that are most endearing and beautiful to us. Forms that convey not only outer beauty, but also inward perfection.

Tethering this incident back to Jesus, Mary, and the Christian community generally, Ibn al-ʿArabi states that the followers of Jesus are attracted to statues and images because of the overwhelming power of the handsome form that the holy spirit appeared to Mary. Thenceforth, the physical image continued to exercise power on Christ's miracle performance and, in turn, the Christian fascination with images. This became a mediating channel to presence God.

"Every great artist gives birth to a new universe, in which the familiar things look the way they have never before looked to anyone."
– Rudolph Arnheim, *Art and Visual Perception*

The Muslim mystic then explains that the reason why the Muslim community was forbidden from such external and physical form making is not, as many legal scholars explain, because it is forbidden. Rather, this was to liberate our ethereal imagination from its physical prison. The Sufi lens through which Ibn al-ʿArabi reads Islam transforms physical beauty into familiar metaphors that breathe life in the precious meanings residing in our hidden treasure.

We continue in the next chapter to discuss *al-haqiqa al-muhammadiyya* (The Muhammadan Reality), where the artist becomes art. We conclude this section with another solemn contemplation: our creative process is a sacred meeting between the external macrocosm, internal microcosm, and the divine metacosm. We are all predisposed to <u>adapt</u> and <u>adopt</u> divine creativity, whether knowingly or unknowingly. Those of us who are conscious of this primordial <u>mission</u> have the beautiful responsibility of delivering the <u>missive</u> to the rest of humanity.

Al-Haqiqa al-Muhammadiyya: **On Artist as Art**

"My ally is the Force, and a powerful ally it is. Life creates it, makes it grow. Its energy surrounds us, binds us. Luminous beings are we, not this crude matter. You must feel the Force flow around you. Here, between you, me, the tree, the rock"
– Master Yoda, Star Wars: The Empire Strikes Back

What exactly is creative inspiration? Is it an idea, emotion, movement, or energy? What does it taste or feel like? We learned in the previous chapter that creative inspiration arrives in different theatrical plays, some more flamboyant than others. Sometimes as a galloping horse, other moments as silence. But now, given our appreciation of the metaphysics of the creative process and its birth in the deepest precipices of the unseen, we should distinguish between how creative inspiration manifests in our physical world (*nasut*) and what it looks like backstage.

Ibn al-ʿArabi gives us an insight into his own creative process, which in his case might be alternatively called a 'mystical opening'. It is one of my convictions, one that I hope this book will elucidate and affirm, that what we term the creative process and mystical experience are one and the same journey, simply two sides of the same coin; a mirror that reflects upon itself, <u>constantly</u> and <u>incessantly</u>.

The Sufi sage speaks of his creative mystical experience that would eventually manifest in his magnum opus, *The Meccan Openings*, as a vision that he had during a ritual pilgrimage to Mecca, while circumambulating the Kaaba. He suddenly witnessed an apparition that he named *al-fata al-fa'it* (the elapsed youth). Like the prophet Muhammad ﷺ and countless other sages throughout history, God often appears in the form of a 'beardless youth'. The importance of this image, or corporeal metaphor, is less so in the form and more in the innocence that is associated with young age.

> *"A successful work of art is not one which resolves contradictions in a spurious harmony, but one which expresses the idea of harmony negatively by embodying the contradictions, pure and uncompromised, in its innermost structure."*
> – Theodore Adorno

Ibn al-ʿArabi describes this 'elapsed youth' in contradictory terms, as the living dead, silent speaker, and simple composite. He utilizes the same language in his litanies whilst describing the perplexing nature of existence:

> A permeating divine identity, unique appearances, existence and non-existence, light and darknesses, hearing and deafness, tablet and pen, ignorance and knowledge, war and peace, silence and utterance, closure and opening, reality and truth, a pre-eternal unseen, an eternal continuity.

This is a common spirit present in many spiritual traditions and their perception of ultimate reality. Ibn al-ʿArabi often quotes an earlier Muslim saint Abu Saʿid al-Kharraz, who when asked: "Where did you find God?" He replied: "At the meeting of opposites." Henry Corbin, in his beautiful exposition on Ibn al-ʿArabi's thought, *Alone with the Alone*, references this statement in relation to the similar notion in Christian mysticism known as *coincidentia oppositorum*.

Returning to the Muslim mystic's encounter with *al-fata al-faʾit*, Ibn al-ʿArabi faints, due to the magnitude of this vision, and when he awakens asks the elapsed youth to gift him a secret, which he says arrived as a singular *maʿna* (meaning) that was cast upon his heart. Over the course of the next 30 years, this unfurled into a procession of *suwar* (images): a voluminous work known as *The Meccan Openings*. Ibn al-ʿArabi explains that this is one of two ways in which divine inspiration arrives to the heart of the seeker: either as a meaning or image.

> *"The spirit of creation is simply the spirit of contradiction."*
> – Jean Cocteau

In the first instance, just as the Muslim mystic had received *The Meccan Openings*, a meaning will essentially dig a well in the heart of the seeker, then unleash all the images dormant therein. In the second instance, a single form will yield only one <u>word</u> or <u>work</u>. Be that as it may, Ruth Stone's account of her creative inspiration coming towards her as a galloping horse reveals that even a meaning may arrive embodied in a corporeal image, much like the Sufi mystic's *al-fata al-faʾit*, an apparition laden with contra-dictions and creative tension.

If this is the method that creative inspiration arrives, the question remains as to its exact composition. Even if we were to agree that it's a muse or spirit, what is the energy and force that moves this entity? For Sufi mystics like Ibn al-ʿArabi, there is a medium that sustains not only mystical experiences and creative inspiration, but the entire fabric of existence. The primordial light of the prophet Muhammad ﷺ is, as mentioned in one of his teachings, "The first thing that God created."

Ibn al-ʿArabi explains in *The Meccan Openings* that *al-haqiqa al-muhammadiyya* (Muhammadan Reality) is what Greek philosophers referred to as *al-ʿaql al-awwal* (the first intellect), otherwise known as *logos*; a concept that migrated from Greek philosophy to Judaism, where it was adapted as the 'pre-eternal law', then to Christianity as the nature of Christ. In turn, the Muslim mystic's deep and rich metaphysics of the prophetic reality establishes a sophisticated understanding of *logos* in Sufism.

"The thing is: It takes a lot of energy to be creative. You don't have that energy if you waste it on other stuff."
– Austin Kleon

Prior to outlining the contours of this concept as it pertains to creativity, I would like to begin by discussing the superiority of the prophet's historical person in Sufism and the innovative symbolism that animates Ibn al-ʿArabi's second most important work, *The Bezels of Wisdom*. Incidentally, this is a book that the author mentions he received, in its entirety, as a gift from the prophet himself in a dream. Truly, the name, content, and organization of this monograph embodies Ibn al-ʿArabi's mystical creativity.

The title of the book in Arabic *Fusus al-Hikam* is rich in meaning. A *fass* (bezel) is the engraving on a *khatam* (ring) wherein fits a gemstone. Each chapter of the book is dedicated to a prophet/sage whose life and mission represents a particular spiritual archetype. For example, the chapter dedicated to Jesus is titled: "The Bezel of a Prophetic Wisdom in a Christic Word." Despite the fact that the book does not overall follow a linear chronology of prophets according to sacred Islamic history, the first and last chapters do follow this sequence and are focused on Adam and Muhammad ﷺ, respectively.

> *"The collective unconscious consists of the sum of the instincts and their correlates, the archetypes. Just as everybody possesses instincts, so he also possesses a stock of archetypal images."*
> – Carl Jung

There is a deep co-incidence between the word *khatam* (ring) and the status of the prophet ﷺ as *khatim al-nubuwwa* (seal of prophethood), meaning the last prophet who was given a *shari'a* (law) sent to humanity, according to Islamic creed. The ring symbol also vividly emerges in an *athar* where the prophet ﷺ states that the 'black stone', a holy relic engraved in the Ka'ba and believed to have descended from heaven, is a ring on the right hand of God; whoever kisses it has embraced the divine's right hand.

The prophet's cousin, Ali, is also narrated to have mentioned that God had fed the black stone all the covenants that human beings had made with Him in the realm of spirits: to believe and worship Him. On the Day of Judgment, this relic will testify for – or against – people as to the way they lived and fulfilled their covenants. From God to the prophet and humanity, the black stone returns us to a similar series of mirrorings that we explored in previous chapters between microcosm, macrocosm, and metacosm.

The other motif that undergirds the prophetic primordial reality and the mystical engine that animates *The Bezels of Wisdom* is the prophet's description as 'the walking Qur'an'. Ibn al-'Arabi refers to this in *The Meccan Openings*, recounting a conversation between the prophet's wife 'A'isha who was asked by a Muslim about the character of God's messenger. She responded: "Do you not recite the Qur'an? His character was the Qur'an", and in other narrations, she is reported to have said: "He was a walking Qur'an."

"I chose faces and figures as my subject matter simply due to the fact that the human form is already beautiful art."
– Frank Bruno

The Sufi mystic comments that any Muslim who did not live during the prophet's time and desires to see him need only look at scripture; it is as if the Qur'an was embodied in a human form known as Muhammad b. 'Abdullah ﷺ. He even goes further by stating that since the Qur'an, as divine speech, is an attribute of God, so is Muhammad a divine characteristic, further cementing the intimate mirroring between the prophet, God, and creation.

One of the prophet's companions affirms his taste of this symbolism when he mentions that he had seen the prophet the last day before his passing and that his face was like a page from the Qur'an. Artistic praises of the prophet's perfect form reiterate this sentiment as well. For instance, we find that 'Abdul-Rahman al-Dayba'i, the author of a *mawlid* (celebration of the prophet's birth), poetically describes the facial features of God's viceroy as such: "His nose is like the letter *alif* (ا); his mouth like the letter *mim* (ـم); his eyebrows like the letter *nun* (ن)."

The lady saint ʿAmina ʿAdil also mentions a mythological imagining of the beginning of creation, in the primordial realm of spirits when the aforementioned covenants were taken from the souls of all human beings and fed to the black stone. There, the author mentions, human souls perceived different aspects of the perfected Muhammadan form. Those who saw his hands were destined to become artists. Specifically, the ones who witnessed his palms would become calligraphers; whereas those who witnessed his shadow became musicians.

> *"Perhaps the mission of an artist is to interpret beauty to people - the beauty within themselves."*
> – Langston Hughes

Here we see the first glimpses of the concordance between artist and art in Sufism, embodied perfectly and completely in the person of the prophet ﷺ. He is the consummate divine work of art whose beauty, in turn, inspires other artists but whose primordial light is itself creative inspiration. The Muhammadan light and its pertinence to creativity in Sufism is a concept still relevant today, as one of the prominent contemporary American Muslim scholars Dr. Umar Abdullah mentioned once that any beauty one perceives in the world is, at root, the beauty and light of the prophet.

Returning back to *The Bezels of Wisdom*, Ibn al-ʿArabi thoroughly imprints the Qurʾanic image of the prophet in this book. Just as the Islamic scripture was revealed in stages, 23 years to be exact, so was the prophet ﷺ also 'revealed' in each of the different prophets and messengers throughout history. Adam, considered the first messenger in Islam, was a manifestation of the perfected human form that God had created with His own two hands. More than that, Adam could be considered the 'revelation' of the prophet Muhammad's own body. One may even call the prophet of Islam's soma Adam.

And so is the case with the prophet Idris (Enoch) who represents Muhammadan knowledge; Moses who symbolizes majesty and Jesus who is seen as a mirror of the Word embodied in human form. Christ, in this sacred history, is the penultimate and most crucial stage before the complete synthesis of God's project to manifest His perfect attributes in the mirror of *al-insan al-kamil al-tamm* (the perfect and complete human). The reason why the prophet of Islam, and the Qur'an, appeared in stages is that the uni-verse(s) can only bear the weight of such a manifestation if it appears gradually, not all at once.

> *"I respect everything in change and the solemn beauty of life and death... and therefore, while man is amidst the immense beauty of objective bodies, he must possess the capacity of self-perfection and must observe and represent his world with full confidence."*
> – Ansel Adams

The prophet Muhammad ﷺ, as *al-insan al-kamil al-tamm*, is the perfected and completed mirror within which God may reflect upon His names and attributes. Here, there are three questions that require elucidation. First, what is the difference between perfection and completion. Second, how does a human being engage with and manifest God's attributes. Lastly, how does this vision apply to artists and the creative process?

To address the first point, Ibn al-ʿArabi explains that *kamal* (perfection) is to reach the highest standard of a certain trait or characteristic (i.e., *tawba* [repentance], *sabr* [patience], *rida* [contentment]). The journey to reach these stations is gradual and cumulative. Throughout history, Muslim mystics have delineated the journey towards truth according to these different *maqamat* (permanent spiritual stations), usually beginning with repentance and ending with contentment, and their corresponding *ahwal* (transitory spiritual states).

"The same feeling of not belonging, of futility, wherever I go: I pretend interest in what matters nothing to me, I bestir myself mechanically or out of charity, without ever being caught up, without ever being somewhere. What attracts me is elsewhere, and I don't know where that elsewhere is."
— Emil M. Cioran, *The Trouble with Being Born*

Ibn al-ʿArabi adds another station above contentment, that of *qurba* (nearness). He explains that once a seeker begins to experience fleeting breezes or *ahwal* (states) of an imminent *maqam* (station), such as — for example — a sense of regret that is a trace of repentance, this is a sign that they will soon reach that station. Once they obtain this status, it becomes <u>a part</u> of their imprint, never to leave them <u>apart</u>. Then, the cycle continues with states foreshadowing another station that is to come. This process continues until one reaches the highest rank of nearness.

However, Ibn al-ʿArabi explains that once all these traits have been perfected, the seeker aspires to reach yet another higher and paradoxical place known as *maqam al-la maqam* (station of no-station). It is called thus because, at that point, the seeker has achieved perfect attention to all the previous stations, manifesting all their associated traits in equilibrium without one seeking his or her attention more than the other, hence the name 'station of no station'.

As for <u>completion</u>, which <u>complements</u> perfection, it is the ability to appreciate the struggles of those who have not yet reached the highest standard in any particular station. This is a necessary aesthetic <u>sensitivity</u> and <u>sensibility</u> to appreciate beauty in all things, even those that we have been accustomed to regard as ugly. Simply, completion teaches that there is a potential <u>beatific</u> <u>beauty</u> in all things.

> *"The job of art is to chase ugliness away."*
> – Bono, U2

This was a central principle in Ibn al-ʿArabi's own life. Claude Addas' mentions a story in her biographical work on the Sufi mystic, titled *Quest for the Red Sulfur*, where during the early years of his *suluk* (self-discipline), while studying under an Andalusian sage named Abu-l-ʿAbbas al-ʿUraybi, the former developed a habit of carrying a foul-smelling dead fish with him wherever he went. Although his teacher had no problem with this practice, the other students became concerned for their friend and peer.

They complained to al-ʿUraybi that although Ibn al-ʿArabi means well by carrying this fish as a means to discipline his ego, it might reflect negatively on the image of his family and father specifically who was a well-known diplomat. Their teacher smiled, since he knew of Ibn al-ʿArabi's true intention and instructed his students to speak to the young mystic directly about their concern.

When his friends expressed their opinion, Ibn al-ʿArabi explained that the reason he carried this dead fish was not to humiliate, but rather honor himself. He believed with conviction that God would not have allowed this carcass to continue to exist in the physical world if it were not fit to be a vessel for His manifestations. In other words, it is not only human beings who are struggling with impatience, anger, or sin, but even animals, plants and minerals that should receive *al-insan al-kamil al-tamm*'s mercy, reverence, and reference.

Elsewhere, in *The Meccan Openings*, Ibn al-ʿArabi specifically speaks about the superiority of animals by referencing their description in Arabic as *baha'im* (sing. *bahima*, 4-legged beast). Utilizing his creativity etymology, the Sufi mystic connects this word to the divine presence of *bahamut* (obfuscation). This is a comparable realm to *lahut*, discussed in the previous chapter, but one that focuses on the inability of human rationality to comprehend the divine communication emanating at that level of reality.

"If you talk to the animals, they will talk with you, and you will know each other. If you do not talk to them, you will not know them and what you do not know, you will fear. What one fears, one destroys."
– Chief Dan George, Tsleil-Waututh Nation

And so, Ibn al-ʿArabi states that the reason animals are described as *baha'im* is not as a denigration, but rather to ennoble them as a creation of God that understands and utters spiritual realities that are inaccessible to human beings. The Sufi mystic finds a proof for this in the Qur'anic verse: "The seven heavens glorify Him, so does the earth and whatever is in it, but you do not comprehend their glorification" (17:44). This is also embodied in the lives of many Muslim sages who received wisdom and teachings from lions, fish, and other animals.

Moving to the second point, concerning the manner in which human beings engage with divine manifestations, Ibn al-ʿArabi provides a detailed explanation of the <u>constant</u> flux between the vowels and <u>consonants</u> of our existence, both as mirrors in which God reflects upon His names and attributes. The Sufi mystic states that at any given point in time, the human being has a responsibility towards three different divine names: that which is exercising power over us, a second to which we are transitioning, and third that seeks to engage with us, but will ultimately not do so. Rather, it is bound to be a mere <u>fleeting</u> <u>meeting</u>.

"Only the man who has had to face despair is really convinced that he needs mercy. Those who do not want mercy, never seek it. It is better to find God on the threshold of despair than to risk our lives in a complacency that has never felt the need of forgiveness."
– Thomas Merton, *No Man is an Island*

These divine names fall into one of two categories: *jamal* (beauty) (e.g., mercy, clemency, forgiveness, innovation) or *jalal* (majesty) (e.g., vengefulness, pride, subduing, overwhelming). In general, the <u>*adab*</u> (etiquette) that one should have with the first set of names is to <u>feast</u> on that <u>*maʾduba* (feast)</u> and clothe oneself in those traits. As for the second, one should be in awe and not <u>dress</u> themselves in that <u>dress</u>. Like reading <u>*adab*</u> (literature), as Hemingway insists, one should seek to understand a character's faults, but in everyday life, one should neither agree nor embody such vices.

These names of *jamal* and *jalal* show their effects on our lives in phases of *bast* (expansion) and *qabd* (constriction), *yusr* (ease) and *ʿusr* (difficulty), exhalation and inhalation, suffering and redemption, and the overarching ebb and flow of life. The Qurʾan provides a succinct framework as to how this create-ive cycle moves: "Indeed, with every difficulty there is ease. Indeed, with every difficulty there is ease" (94:5). As mother nature goes through seasons, so do we in body, mind, and spirit.

The *adab* (etiquette) that we should have with the divine name that is currently exercising power over us, be it *jamal* or *jalal*, expansion or ease, is to <u>dress</u> or <u>redress</u> ourselves accordingly. The same applies to the divine attribute to which we are transitioning and even that which although is a fleeting visitor still demands our attention. As these cycles continue to flourish and whither, we learn about God, the universe, and ultimately ourselves.

> *"Ever watch somebody who doesn't know you're watching them? An old woman sitting on a bus? Or kids going to school? Somebody just waiting, and you see this flash come over them. And you know immediately that has nothing to do with anything external because that hasn't changed. They're just sort of realer and more alive. You look at someone long enough, you discover their humanity."*
> – Simon Bishop, *As Good As It Gets*

We should clarify that these interactions with the divine names need not be extraordinary events. It appears as coffee and its breathtaking aroma that we drink in the morning that seems to embrace and halt time, or that driver next to us who is in a road-rage and almost causes a head-on collision, or maybe the epiphany that comes to you as you watch a cat chase a mouse down the street, or a coworker who is just having a bad day and decides to share it with you generously by screaming, yelling or any other creative way to make you miserable.

Remembering our conversation in the first chapter, on storytelling, we <u>acknowledge</u> the <u>knowledge</u> that nothing within or without us is mundane, unless we do not pay enough attention to it. Rather, everyone and everything is sacred and enchanted if we are careful enough to include it as a thread in the stories we weave; the distinct ones we call art and smaller tales we exhale and inhale in our imagination. We are each <u>living a myth</u>, nay <u>a living myth</u>, one in which we are both protagonist and antagonist, depending on how we <u>perceive</u> and <u>receive</u> the <u>gifts</u> or <u>rifts</u> that arrive at our shore.

We come to the third question, regarding how Ibn al-ʿArabi's vision of *al-insan al-kamil al-tamm*, the perfection and completion of engaging with divine names and attributes applies to the creative process. We have already seen glimpses of the 'artist as art' in the person of the prophet ﷺ who is considered by Muslim sages to be not only perfected divine art, but also the source of inspiration for all artists and creative souls.

"Every child is born an artist. The trick is how to remain an artist once we grow up."
– Pablo Picasso

The first reflection I would like to share is that just as a seeker climbs the ranks of spiritual states and stations, towards *maqam al-la maqam*, every artist is also subconsciously ascending towards a singularity with every work they birth in their respective craft. A painter seeks to find a single color, and they will expend moments, hues, and brush strokes to arrive at that dye which their spirit had known as a <u>remembrance</u>, prior to their earthly descent and now seeks to reactivate that <u>memory</u> throughout its bodily journey.

Likewise, every musician seeks their *sawt sarmad* (primordial sound) that Hazrat Inayat Khan mentions, and they are willing to expend all the crescendos and cadences in their soul to reach that shore. Every filmmaker, pottery maker, poet, sculptor, carpenter, martial artist, cook, mother, engineer, and gardener is seeking their place of stillness. And we are truly beautifully broken beings whose triumph resides in our limited set of tools, *bricolage*, that we brilliantly construct out of our constriction and expansion.

As the artist ascends towards their promised scent, they go through three stages that Sufis describe as *ta'alluq* (attachment), *takhalluq* (adornment), and *tahaqquq* (self-realization). First, we attach ourselves to the craft of pen, brush, pick, or chisel through a love and passion that makes us forget time itself. Then, when we stand to depart after a long date-day with our craft, we are already awaiting the next session. It is said that your passion is that which you love to do without any compensation or encouragement. More than this, it is that for which your entire lifetime is not enough to enjoy.

> *"Creativity is allowing yourself to make mistakes. Art is knowing which ones to keep."*
> – Scott Adams

Then comes *takhalluq*, when and where one begins to hear their craft speak to them from beyond the body, not in color, sound, or word but in silence and stillness. The form of our art begins to possess and obsess us. We hear the music before it begins, can read the poem and visualize the curvature of its letters before the first breath, and almost taste the dye as it ages under the gaze of artist and audience. Our medium becomes the language we speak inwardly, whereas outwardly we are merely translators trying to explain to the world our inner word.

Lastly, comes *tahaqquq*, where the artist finally becomes art. This is when a painter is performing with their 'I'. You see all the past, <u>present</u>, and future works in their <u>eyes</u> when they speak, while you are awed by their <u>presence</u>. I had such an experience once when I met one of my oud idols, the Palestinian musician Simon Shaheen, a true virtuoso of his craft. As I stood in front of him, for the first time, I could feel his two wings of oud and violin carry the entire heritage of Arabic music, including Riyad al-Sunbati, Farid al-Atrash and Muhammad Abdul Wahab, as he soared beyond the grammar of the Arabic language to its spirit, felt by everyone through his music.

> *"Creativity is seeing what others see and thinking what no one else ever thought."*
> – Albert Einstein

Who is the 'perfect and complete artist' but a spotless mirror that reflects its hidden treasure with such purity that one wonders whether they are perceiving the ocean itself or simply a reflection, otherwise known as the shore. As we will see in a later chapter, on the *shari'a* (law), *tariqa* (path), and *haqiqa* (reality) of the craft, a 'perfect and complete artist' is hardly one who never makes mistakes, but rather one for whom every mistake is a <u>beatific</u> vision, an opportunity for *jamal* (<u>beauty</u>) to <u>breathe</u>.

The 18th Moroccan Sufi saint 'Abdul 'Aziz al-Dabbagh mentions a story about a sage who while walking in the street one day saw a cat cleaning itself. This was the channel through which he received his *fath* (mystical opening), at which point he let out a loud cry and fainted. Just like Ruth Stone's poem came in the form of a galloping horse, so do sages of all forms also receive their gifts in what appears to be so mundane amidst their surroundings. Art and mysticism agree that the enchanted need not be <u>extraordinary</u>, just <u>ordinary</u> in an <u>exceptional</u> way.

Another sage of his craft, the photographer Richard Misrach, is described by his wife as someone who laughs and enjoys spending time with his family, until his craft calls to him with a prospective scene ready to be admired. At that moment, he completely forgets his surroundings and 'faints' into the enchanted world slumbering in his lens. Nothing is mundane for Misrach; everything is a possibility. And yet, he need not struggle to find these enchanted <u>words</u> in his <u>world</u>. He need only be <u>silent</u> and <u>listen</u>.

"All great art is a visual form of prayer."
– Wendy Beckett

In a remarkable parallel, the prophet's ﷺ daughter Fatima gives an almost exact description of her father when the time came for prayer. He would regularly <u>play</u> and laugh with his family, but as soon as the call to <u>prayer</u> arrives, he forgets about his surroundings and turns his attention singularly upon the window to the unseen that has arrived at his shore. Also, for Misrach and every artist, the craft is itself prayer.

The prophet ﷺ has two important teachings about prayer. In the first, he states that "the entire earth has been made for me a *masjid*." Although this term is often – wrongly – rendered as 'mosque', it literally means the place of prostration. In the second, he states that "the praying person is closest to his lord during prostration." Lastly, there is an often-repeated teaching in Sufism that prayer is the ascension of the believer. Just as the prophet ﷺ ascended above seven heavens, reaching the divine presence, so do the different positions of *salat* (prayer) in Islam also allow for a similar spiritual journey towards God.

In this case, prostration represents that highest station in ascension, when one is admitted into the divine presence. Using those terms that we discussed in the previous chapter; we can say that prostration symbolizes our inner *lahut* and hidden treasure. Since the entire earth has been rendered and enchanted as a place of prostration, everything in this <u>world</u> is a <u>word</u> exhaling its way towards us, awaiting our inhalation.

Like Misrach and the sage in Morocco, as artists we need to always <u>expect</u> the <u>exceptional</u>. Our struggles in this journey should not be seen as a direct catalyst for results, but rather a shaman dance to appease God and our inner *lahut*, that hidden treasure and creative <u>block</u> to <u>unlock</u>. We tell stories through our poems, paintings, and music to makes sense of ourselves and the world around us. And as each work completes its cycle, it points the direction towards others, all the way to *maqam al-la maqam* and our ultimate destination: artists as art.

> *"I saw the angel in the marble and carved until I set him free."*
> – Michelangelo

Before writing my imaginative autobiography, *Souk of Nostalgia*, I had asked one of my spiritual guides Shaykh Hisham Kabbani for grace to write a book about the reality of Sufism. He <u>graciously</u> <u>granted</u> me that and said it would be beneficial. As soon as I began to write, I discovered that I was merely retracing my steps all the way back to childhood. The reality of Sufism is nothing but the Sufism of realities, as I had experienced and lived it.

I deciphered a few important facts about myself through this prayer, which I did not know beforehand. First, I neither recollect nor care much for people from my past, only the aging walls and abodes that connivingly listened to all our conversations and recorded them with the ink of wrinkles and withered textures. Perhaps the brick and mortar already knew of the impending Gulf War that would engulf Iraq; it screamed its way into old age as we naively laughed ourselves into diaspora.

> *"Art is a place where you can be with your own kind, a magical place where imagination flies freely and widely."*
> – Efrat Cybulkiewicz

The second discovery I made is that places from our past, even those physically standing today, are gone. If we are somehow able to bridge that gap of space, separating us from how we remember these buildings, then the abyss of time will always defeat us. My childhood apartment in Baghdad's Haifa street is much bigger in memory, embellished with luster. Its walls speak and sing like one of those magical halls in Tolkien's Middle Earth. Of course, it matters not that this past is now flourishing only in memory and imagination.

The third and most important discovery is that I perceived a pattern in all the places I had lived or visited during my childhood. From Baghdad to Jordan, Senegal to Mecca and Medina, I seem to always tread upon white courtyards of marble. Like subtly placed bastions, they were forgotten until I had recollected them in ink. I wondered about the wisdom behind this motif that was unfolding before my eyes through storytelling. What play was my prayer attempting?

Then, <u>like</u> the crazy artist who <u>likes</u> to make connections where none seem possible or exist, I remembered Ben Affleck's film *Paycheck*, where he portrays an engineer who invents a machine that can predict the future. He eventually becomes a fugitive running away from mercenaries, but not before awakening with his memory erased. He soon realizes that prior to effacing his own past, he had placed clues for himself in the world to know how to survive.

And then it struck me: what if the white courtyards of marble were a clue that my spirit had left for its body just prior to its <u>descent</u>, as a means to assist me in the return journey, the <u>ascent</u>. So much is possible when we are silent and listen to those <u>prostration</u> <u>stations</u> surrounding us. I'm hardly a 'perfect and complete artist', but to at least be aware of what we have to do on this sacred journey, known as creativity, is a first step that is always ready to embrace us, no matter how many times we fail.

The In-Between: On Imagination and Paradox

"Paradoxically though it may seem, it is none the less true that life imitates art far more than art imitates life."
– Oscar Wilde

In the Netflix documentary *Abstract: Art of Design,* the graphic designer Paula Scher explains that when she sits to work every day at the computer in her studio, creative inspiration never arrives. Instead, she finds herself mired in logistical work, responding to emails, marketing, and other non-creative tasks. But then, she goes to the bathroom to fix her lipstick and boom, the creative flood arrives, unannounced.

Like Ruth Stone and countless other artists, Scher is alluding to the elusive nature of creative inspiration. It arrives unannounced but definitely with a pronounced presence. It comes on its own time and will not wait forever. As we saw from Elizabeth Gilbert's unborn story about the Amazon, the interaction between an artist's hidden treasure and an external communication can be severed, whence it will head elsewhere for solace, in another creative <u>soul's</u> embrace. Often, its departure is not due to any fault of our own. Be that as it may, there can be no stillness in this cosmic movement.

Commenting on the Qur'anic verse: "Everyday He is in a different affair" (55:29), Ibn al-'Arabi states unequivocally that there is no repetition in creation. What appears in these uni-verse(s) at any given moment will disappear and never return. In a famous benediction upon the prophet ﷺ, where the author poetically describes the muhammadan reality, he states that it is "the ether of forms that neither appears twice to one person, nor once to two people."

"Repetition is the death of art."
– Robin Green

The Sufi mystic explains that there are two types of non-existence, limited and absolute. The first contains all things that have not come into being but potentially can if God chooses to do so. The second refers to the void where forms go after existing for their moment. They disappear with no possibility of return. What appears after them are similar images that create the illusion of sameness, but in reality, there are never two <u>identical identities</u> in this existence.

Time is an illusory procession, Ibn al-'Arabi tells us; a performance that is born as a result of infinitude attempting to permeate a limited container known as the cosmos. The only possible way for this to happen is for a breeze of manifestations to arrive from limited non-existence, fill this canvas of creation through *nafas al-rahman*, then immediately leave to absolute non-existence, allowing for the next battalion of theophanies to fill our uni-verse(s).

For the Sufi mystic, the reason why there can be no repetition in creation is theologically very simple: to assume repetition is an assault against divine expansiveness, since it implies that God's munificence has depleted and therefore, there is a need to repeat creation and manifestations. The reality of the affair is to the contrary: at every moment there is an entirely new wave from the ocean of *lahut* that arrives at the shore of *nasut*.

> *"The man who suspects his own tediousness is yet to be born."*
> – Thomas Bailey Aldrich

However, Ibn al-ʿArabi states that these newly arriving forms are quite similar to the ones that had just expired, otherwise our witnessing of reality would be utterly frightening and chaotic, whereby at every moment the cosmos changes entirely. The mystic uses this to provide an innovative explanation for boredom, which is to wrongly assume that nothing is changing. If we actually perceived affairs as they are, incessantly fluctuating, we would never find our existence tedious.

Abu Hamid al-Ghazali, another Muslim sage and predecessor of Ibn al-ʿArabi, agrees with him. His definition of a miracle is simply that which is *kharq al-ʿada* (breaking of the habit). The sun rising from the east is no less miraculous than its emergence from the west. However, we have become accustomed to the former phenomenon and therefore regard it as normal. Everything within and without us, our breaths, organs, and dimensions are enchanted miracles, but we have been oppressed to assume otherwise.

As Einstein informed us in the quote mentioned in the previous chapter, creativity is to see what everyone else sees but to think what no one else has. Art is precisely the saintly lens through which we may perceive the miraculous amidst the ordinary, the <u>exceptional</u> within the <u>expected</u>, and the *yusr* (ease) through the *'usr* (difficulty). This is all synonymous with our ongoing definition of art and creativity in this book as translating the ineffable into the tangible and making connections where none seem possible or exist.

"Art is a sense of magic."
– Stan Brakhage

To focus on the notion of *hayra* (perplexity), and the arrival of creative inspiration when least expected, the French philosopher Jacques Derrida gives a poignant comparison between two senses of future in French, *le futur* and *l'avenir*. The former refers to an expected and predictable future: our plans to go to the doctor, have a vacation or meet with friends. This, Derrida says, is not the real future. It is like a work of art that has a few imprisoned meanings caged by an oppressive artist. It cannot live outside this tyranny.

Instead, Derrida states that the real sense of future is *l'avenir*, which is 'the arrival', that which is so looming that it tethers itself to the present moment. It is completely unexpected, entirely here and now. This is a guest who tells you to prepare for their visit, but ultimately arrives unannounced, on their own terms. The <u>host</u> must always be prepared without <u>hostility</u>. Their <u>presence</u> and <u>prescience</u> are necessary yet futile in the grand scheme of foretelling the <u>imminent immanence</u> of what is to come.

We should ask, why does creative inspiration that is every artist's *l'avenir* arrive unannounced? What is the wisdom behind this paradoxical and perplexing journey where our hard work does not correlate directly with our creative expansiveness? Once we understand and appreciate that the source of these *nafis* (precious) gems is otherworldly, from that inner *lahut* otherwise known as the hidden treasure, we can perceive the wisdom in this fragile process.

> *"Inspiration is for amateurs. The rest of us just show up and get to work. If you wait around for the clouds to part and a bolt of lightning to strike you in the brain, you are not going to make an awful lot of work. All the best ideas come out of the process; they come out of the work itself."*
> – Chuck Close

When we say unexpected, it might seem as though we are also implying irrational or illogical, since our minds are trained to think that any action (e.g., struggle or hard work) has a specific reaction (e.g., growth and creative inspiration). However, in reality, this paradox is not irrational but supra-rational, functioning according to a higher order of 'sense'. It is to let us know, with conviction, that the source of our creativity is not us, or at least not our material dimension, but rather the spiritual and beyond.

As mentioned previously, we can think of the interplay between our hard work as artists, which is under our control, and the presence – or absence – of creative inspiration as a dance between *yusr* (ease) and *'usr* (difficulty), *bast* (expansion) and *qabd* (constriction). On the days when the 'flow' of creative inspiration is present, it is our responsibility to be good hosts for our *l'avenir* guest, not only because it will not stay forever, perhaps even tell other artists about what lousy hosts we are as Gilbert eloquently expresses, but also because we owe this attention to our inner *lahut* and hidden treasure, for our own sake.

On the other hand, when those days of creative <u>ebb</u> come and we find ourselves caught in the <u>web</u> of constriction, those are the cycles during which we also need to work in order to show *shukr* (gratitude), acknowledging all prior visitations from our creative inspiration and appeasing for it to return. We ride the <u>wave</u> during the flow of the ocean but continue to <u>wade</u> and <u>wait</u> nonetheless during the ebb, for the next rush of energy.

"He who works with his hands is a laborer. He who works with his hands and head is a craftsman. He who works with his hands, head and heart is an artist."
— St. Francis of Assisi

In Arabic, as Ibn al-ʿArabi has shown us, linguistic structures like anagrams (two words that have the same letters arranged differently), homonyms (words that have identical spelling and pronunciation but different meanings), and contranyms (words that have identical spelling and pronunciation but opposite meanings) play a tremendous role in poetic play and, in the Muslim mystic's case, a metaphor in <u>ink</u> signaling a metaphysical <u>link</u>.

The word *shukr* (gratitude) is a poignant example, for its anagram *shirk* (polytheism) is considered the worst sin in the Islamic creed. Even though the term theologically means to worship other gods beside God, what does it actually refer to in relationship to gratitude and the artist's responsibility towards their creative inspiration? If *shukr* is to acknowledge the source of all bounties to be the divine *lahut*, the metacosmic hidden treasure, then *shirk* is to assume the opposite: that anything other than this ultimate origin is where our inspiration is born.

For artists, we do not work because the inspiration is present, as painter Chuck Close mentions, for it is not the ultimate source of our creativity. In turn, if we stop working when it is not there, then we fit the description of the false Sufi: those who are *'abd al-hal* (slave of the spiritual state). This is someone who only prays and worships when they 'feel like it'. We do not go to work, be good to our families and friends only when we are happy to do so, so why would we abuse our talents as artists and work only when it is enjoyable?

"In the universe, there are things that are known, and things that are unknown, and in between them, there are doors."
– William Blake, *The Marriage of Heaven and Hell*

For Ibn al-'Arabi, both *hayra* (perplexity) of the unexpected *arrival* and *khayal* (imagination) of the artist are interrelated. Rather, each is a mirror of the other, much like the human being reflects the uni-verse(s), all of which in turn reflect God. Moreover, as we explained earlier in this chapter, the Sufi mystic tethers these two notions to the muhammadan reality, which is the cosmic creative force that we discussed in the previous chapter.

We first introduced *'alam al-khayal* (the realm of imagination) in chapter 2, "The Hidden Treasure", and we highlighted that Ibn al-'Arabi names it *jabarut* (dominion), the liminal world between *malakut* (kingdom) – of spirits – and *nasut* (physical world). This liminality of *khayal* (imagination) is central in the Sufi mystic's writings. He goes as far as saying that this entire cosmos is nothing but a hierarchy of things and between each pair there is a *barzakh* (liminal interstice).

The reason for the existence of this intermediary realm is central to our conversation here on creativity. As Ibn al-ʿArabi poetically describes *ʿalam al-khayal*, it is one where spirits are corporealized and bodies are spiritualized. By their very nature, *arwah* (spirits) are non-dimensional and purely subtle, hence they cannot appear in the physical world. Inversely, *ajsad* (physical bodies) are dense and three dimensional, and therefore have no access to the spiritual realm.

> *"The intersection of the timeless with time, that is an occupation for the saint."*
> – T.S. Eliot, *Dry Salvages*

Like all of his metaphysical ventures, Ibn al-ʿArabi roots his journey to *khayal* squarely within the Qurʾan. Specifically, this verse: "He merged the two seas, they meet. Between them is a *barzakh* [interstice], they do not transgress" (55:19) is all he needs to construct his expansive vision of imagination, both internal and external to the human being. On the one hand, he extends this verse's literal description of a natural phenomenon, concerning the meeting between fresh and salty waters that takes place in the realm of *nasut*, to a metaphorical prism for the meeting between the fresh water of *malakut* (spiritual realm) and salty water of *nasut* (physical realm) at the *barzakh* (interstice) of *jabarut* (dominion) and *khayal* (realm of imagination).

But he goes even further – for our benefit – by refracting this analogy from the macrocosmic <u>world</u> to the <u>word</u> of the microcosm, the human being who necessarily reflects these cosmic movements and miracles. In this case, Ibn al-ʿArabi posits the human *jasad* (body) to be our inner salty water, the *ruh* (spirit) as the inner fresh water, and the *nafs* (soul) to be the *barzakh* in-between them. This creative mirroring helps immensely in understanding our *suluk* (journey of self-discipline).

Our *nafs* (soul), as we saw in the first chapter, is the seat of our hidden treasure, the *hayr* (fortress) of *hayra* (perplexity) where our *nafis* (precious) meanings reside until the <u>block</u> is <u>unlocked</u> and they are allowed to sail across our *anfas* (pl. breaths) and be externalized as art. This soul, Ibn al-ʿArabi states, is also the private quarters of all our faculties, including the five senses, memory, imagination, and rational reflection.

> *"I am a spirit, and this is naught but flesh,*
> *It was my abode and my garment for a time.*
> *I am a treasure, by a talisman kept hid,*
> *Fashioned of dust, which served me as a shrine,*
> *I am a pearl, which has left its shell deserted,*
> *I am a bird, and this body was my cage,*
> *Whence I have now flown forth and it is left as a token,"*
> – Abu Hamid al-Ghazali

By undertaking the journey of *suluk* (self-discipline), a process that we will explore in the next chapter, our *nafs* begins to travel from its motherly abode known as the *jasad* (body) towards the fatherly *ruh* (spirit)[1]. As the soul treks this mountain, it carries on its shoulders all the faculties as well as the body. What this means is that we begin to perceive the physical world as more than decadent matter, but an enchanted presence rooted in the spirit yet branching in a physical dress. This reaches such a saintly stage, equivalent to *maqam al-la maqam* (station of no station), where our bodies

---

[1] Ibn al-ʿArabi in no way holds that the feminine mother is a lower rank than the masculine father. This is evidenced by the fact that in other excerpts he switches the roles of body and spirit to be father and mother, respectively.

are no longer bound by time and space; they have been liberated from *nasut* and reside in *malakut*, despite outward corporeality.

Fortunately for us, Ibn al-ʿArabi states, if we choose to neglect our *suluk* (self-discipline), whence our souls will take the opposite descent towards the body and unfettered materiality, our spirits will remain stationary, as a reminder of our <u>memory</u> and <u>remembrance</u>. If the spirit, that dimension of ours that is closest to our hidden treasure, were to forget its place in the ocean, then I – for instance – would not have been able to reflect on white courtyards of marble, those spiritual traces marked by textured vestiges throughout my life in diaspora.

> *"Did I not kill you?' Yes, you killed me. And like you, I forgot to die."*
> – Mahmoud Darwish, *In Jerusalem*

The ex-atheist Egyptian Muslim thinker Mostafa Mahmoud provides a poignant analogy of this marriage between memory and spirit. He would like us to imagine ourselves sitting in a car that is driving smoothly on a frictionless road, our only proof of movement are the stationary trees and surroundings that breeze behind us as we tread onwards. Similarly, our spirits are stationary trees that allow us to perceive the changes our bodies undergo, such as aging and the accumulating <u>files</u> from our <u>life</u>, known as memories.

It is not a lost coincidence also that when flying in a plane, at a high altitude, we experience the illusion of being stationary, since the <u>ground</u> beneath us is so far away, that we sometimes lose track of our <u>grounding</u>. Likewise, when we are either immersed entirely in our physicality or spirituality, we temporarily forget our other dimensions, feeling as though our bodies or spirits are timeless. However, the marriage of body and spirit should reside not only in stillness, but also movement.

In one of his most memorable expressions, Ibn al-ʿArabi says: "Reality is *hayra* [perplexity]. Perplexity is anxiety and movement, and movement is life." Returning to the Qurʾan, we find the following verse eloquently embracing the Sufi mystic's expression: "The sun runs towards its place of stillness" (36:38). Lest I am assumed to shallowly use modern science as a proof for theology, we now know that our entire solar system is carried by the sun, much like our *nafs* lifts its faculties and body, as it essentially drills its way through space.

> *"In art, as music, there are rhythms, movements, flow and ebb…"*
> – Betty Jean Billups

The sun gives off heat and light, as do our bodies, while it undertakes its continuous 'physical exercise' all towards the moment when it will be liberated from this outer shell, much like al-Ghazali took off the clothing of <u>flesh</u> for a <u>lush</u> soaring spirit. Ibn al-ʿArabi perceives this principle, the centrality of movement, as permeating even the minute rulings in *shariʿa* (Islamic law). This is why, for example, the water used in *wuduʾ* (ritual ablution) must be running – as opposed to still – water. Not only does still water carry filth, but it is more importantly spiritually dead.

The *barzakh*, that liminal space in-between the body, spirit, and all things also has a unique character. Ibn al-ʿArabi tells us that it must be truly impartial, allowing for a hospitable meeting between two guests that would otherwise not be able to <u>convene</u> or <u>converse</u>. In order for this to happen, the *barzakh* has to have an imprint similar to *maqam al-la maqam*, namely that it should be characterized by both sides between which it resides, yet not be described as either one more than the other.

As mentioned, the Sufi mystic states that the archetype of the *barzakh* fills the cosmos, not only the macrocosmic *jabarut* that corresponds to our inner *nafs* (soul) and resides between our body and spirit, but there is also a liminal threshold between all pairs of things around us, where magical meetings happen. If that is the case, then any two things must necessarily be <u>oppositional</u> in some sense, in order for their *barzakh* to harmonize them as <u>appositional</u>.

> *"Without dreams the artist would perish. Dreams are the initial catalysts which launch us into a position of faith that tells us we can accomplish that which is not already done."*
> – Roger Aisselin

This hierarchical matrix of *barazikh* (pl. *barzakh*) extends at the highest level to the muhammadan reality, which Ibn al-ʿArabi describes as *barzakh al-barazikh* (the liminal of all liminals), or the greatest threshold. This entails that everything in the universe is an in-between and - more importantly – an instance of *khayal* (imagination). Everything and everyone, us included, are dreams of God.

When I was studying French, a language that Derrida has taught me is as rich etymologically as Arabic, I composed the following reflection: 'nous sommes le <u>rêve</u> de dieu. S'il se <u>réveille</u>, tout est fini !' (We are God's dream. If He awakens, then all is finished). Here, I do not insinuate the traditional sense of sleeping, lest any Muslim readers accuse me of heresy implying that God sleeps. Rather, I intend to show that, as Shakespeare mentions, "we are such stuff as dreams are made on, and our life is rounded with a sleep".

Ibn al-ʿArabi delves deeper still into the relationship between imagination and dreams, explaining that the macrocosmic realm of *khayal* (*jabarut*) corresponds to the imaginative faculty in the microcosmic human being. The former is called *al-khayal al-munfasil* (disjointed imagination), since it is <u>apart</u> from the human being, while the latter is *al-khayal al-muttasil* (conjoined imagination), because it is <u>a part</u> of us.

"The line between insanity and mysticism is thin; the line between reality and unreality is thin. Liminality as a spiritual concept is all about the porousness of boundaries."
– Esmé Weijun Wang, *The Collected Schizophrenias: Essays*

When we dream, or have an active imagining, a connection is made between our own *jabarut* (imaginative faculty) and its external cosmic mirror. In *The Meccan Openings*, Ibn al-ʿArabi emphasizes that this tethering is neither exclusive to Muslims nor believers, but rather a universal disposition in all of us: "Every human being who has an imagination, when they imagine, their gaze extends to the presence of divine imagination."

He also emphasizes that it is possible to venture, in a waking state, to the macrocosmic imagination. This external *jabarut* appears to its guests as a wonderland of sorts that is known by at least two names, which Ibn al-ʿArabi excavates directly from the Qurʾan: *ard al-haqiqa* (the land of reality) and *ard Allah al-wasiʿa* (God's vast earth). He states that saints often venture into this land to accomplish spiritual duties delegated to them by God. He even recounts his own marvelous adventures there.

In one of these journeys, he comes across a <u>sea</u> of sand, as far as the eye can <u>see</u>. He then perceived other sages and travelers like him who halted at specific *manazil* (abodes) like train stations, awaiting their transportation. The vehicle arrives and it is a 'ship made of stone'. Its rocks seem attracted to one another like magnets, clinging together to form a large <u>boat</u> which travelers <u>board</u> as they sail towards the horizon. Then, other ships come, and the entire sea of sand is filled with these stations.

This creative vision, which seems like a film scene, is why I believe Ibn al-ʿArabi would express that much of contemporary cinema and television are divinely inspired. This sentiment was expressed explicitly by the 20th West African Sufi saint Ibrahim Niasse who instructed his *murids* (disciples) to watch the cinema of the Europeans because there are glimpses of *haqiqa* (reality) in this craft. This is a topic that we will explore in more detail in a later chapter specifically focused on the moving arts.

"The most powerful words in English are 'Tell me a story,' words that are intimately related to the complexity of history, the origins of language, the continuity of the species, the taproot of our humanity, our singularity, and art itself."
– Pat Conroy

As we discussed earlier, Spielberg makes films that externalize his inner fears and fascinations. He is a sage who continuously listens not only to his hidden treasure but also the macrocosm's voice speaking back to him. He fits Ibn al-ʿArabi's eloquent and loving homage to poets: "They have annihilated their words in existent things. This one writes about women, the other about status, wealth, or honor. But behind all these forms there is only Him."

What the Sufi mystic would like us to know is that our creativity births spirits dressed in corporeal bodies known as words, colors, or sounds. But this much we already knew. It is the imprint of *hayra* (perplexity) upon all the layers of imagination (micro, macro and meta) that requires more of our attention. The Sufi mystic beautifully expresses this in the statement: "From the darknesses of ignorance, to light of guidance, and lastly darkness of perplexity."

The principle that movement is a sign of life applies here. Just as the running water of ablution grants the human body an enlivening energy, so must we constantly wash ourselves with the flow of creativity. We do not stop when a goal is reached. We move the destination just beyond our grasp. Rather, we need to perceive the journey itself of creat-ing as our destination. As John Caputo beautifully states in *On Religion*: "God is not the answer. He is the opening of the question."

> *"The true work of art is but a shadow of the divine perfection."*
> – Michelangelo

To further capitalize on this point, the authors of *Art and Fear* highlight that success might just be the most dangerous thing for an artist; a state that kills their willingness to produce more work. This in no way means that all our poems, paintings, or music have to be failures. It does mean, however, that our focus should be on listening to our creative process as opposed to the work itself. This the authors of the book state explicitly: artists are interested in each other's creative process, whereas everybody else focuses on the product.

If a work of art is the *jasad* (body), then the creative process is the *ruh* (spirit) that is enclothed within. Meanwhile, the artist emerges as the *nafs* (soul), *barzakh* (threshold), and *khayal* (imagination) that hosts both guests in a meeting. The *hayra* (perplexity) in all of this is that both, the creative process and work, are simultaneously the artist and not the artist, just like the universe is God/not God, as Ibn al-ʿArabi tells us.

Gilbert uses a similar analogy as a window into the paradoxical life of art when she addresses the artist-reader and says: "Your art matters/does not matter." It does because it is the most sacred of movements, from your *lahut* to *nasut*. But it also does not because – and this is my explanation – we are neither its <u>creators</u> nor <u>controllers</u>. We are essential to the divine drama if and only if we acknowledge our *lahut* and hidden treasure. Otherwise, we risk mistaking the waves for the ocean, and trees for the forest.

> *"Everyone has the capacity to be innovative and creative in their day-today work –*
> *regardless of your job!"*
> – William Pollard

For Ibn al-ʿArabi, the incessant movement that sustains imagination and perplexity also describes love, which he defines as a lover's longing to union with the beloved. If such a union occurs physically then the object of love changes, from the longing for the union to happen to the desire that it continue indefinitely. Hence, he states, the object of love is never truly achieved. But that is, not unlike creativity, hardly a bad thing. On the contrary, our physical, mental, and spiritual movement is what we truly <u>crave</u>, not <u>closure</u>.

I once asked a friend who happens to be an exquisite saxophone player how he would describe the experience of learning music, a topic that we discuss in a later chapter. He described it like diving into an ocean, whence you reach what seems to be the ocean-bed, only to find it giving beneath you and there is a new depth to explore. Like so, the cycle continues indefinitely. Perplexity, imagination, love, and art are all ultimately different mirrors for the same spirit that animates us, human beings.

Almost every artist who is a sage of their craft concurs that all human beings, whether conscious artists or not, have creativity imprinted in their being. This should not be difficult to accept when we perceive the intimate relationship between imagination and the most emblematic emotion we have as a species, love. A mother's love for her child is nothing but art. Beyond this, however, there is also an artisanship that can be achieved in every discipline, from accounting to engineering.

> *"Anyone who can handle a needle convincingly can make us see a thread which is not there."*
> – E.H. Gombrich, *Art and Illusion*

I would like to end this chapter with a personal story that connects everything we have discussed so far to the two definitions of creativity that we introduced in the preface: to translate the ineffable into the tangible and make connections where none seem possible or exist. Some years ago, I was playing a video game called *Uncharted 3*, an action story that follows the adventures of Nathan Drake, a descendant of 16th century explorer Sir Francis Drake.

In this specific iteration, Nathan is searching for the city of Ur, a wonderland of fanciful treasures that his ancestor had supposedly stumbled upon in *al-rub' al-khali* (Empty Quarter), an unforgiving desert in

Southern Arabia. The city of Ur – a biblical name – also happens to be mentioned in the Qur'an as Iram. As Nathan treads the hot desert, hallucinating from the heat, he eventually finds the city like an illusory mirage that turns out to be a real oasis.

At the same time, I was also reading an Arabic play by Khalil Gibran titled *Iram of the Lofty Pillars*. It is a story about a lady saint, Amina al-ʿAlawiyya, who as a young child used to accompany her father's trade caravan into the Empty Quarter. One day she disappeared in the desert, only to emerge years later as a saint who lives in a forest and is sought by people from across the east and west for her wisdom.

> *"Did you take the forests, like me, as an abode instead of castles? Did you follow the springs, and climbed the rocks?"*
> – Khalil Gibran, *The Entourages*

The play begins with a Christian seeker, Najib Rahma, who arrives in the forest where the lady saint lives. There, he finds Zayn al-ʿAbidin, an advanced Muslim mystic who begins telling Naguib about Amina. Then, when she finally appears to the two men, their conversation delves so deeply into the ocean of metaphysics, the reader might assume they are amidst Ibn al-ʿArabi's own writings, not those of the famed Gibran who wrote a romanticist novel like *The Prophet*.

But it is true, Gibran in Arabic is a much more sophisticated Sufi than his lingering at the shore of English, not due to any shortcoming in the language. But perhaps like me, somewhere between the words and those empty spaces between letters, his native tongue allowed him to return home to Lebanon. Most probably, however, home was as lost for him as

Iram itself; a magical wonderland that exists only in *khayal*. Nevertheless, Gibran was still hopeful. This is why he introduces his play with an epigraph, a statement attributed to the prophet ﷺ: "Some of my community will enter it [Iram]."

> *"Art is the only way to run away without leaving home."*
> – Twyla Tharp

As I played *Uncharted 3* and read *Iram of the Lofty Pillars*, a creative connection emerged in my heart that returned me to scripture. I began reflecting on the single verse where this city is mentioned: "Have you not seen what your Lord has done with ʿAd, *Iram of the Lofty Pillars*, the likes of which was never built in all the lands" (89:6-8). The tribe of ʿAd were the inhabitants of Iram who denied the message of their prophet, Hud. In turn, they were destroyed by God. However, my journey with Nathan Drake and Khalil Gibran made me wonder if the verse hints towards <u>a tribute</u>, not <u>retribution</u>.

Perhaps it is not as many scholars have explained that what God has done with ʿAd is destruction, but instead built through them this city of saints. In this case, I did not feel the need to write a poem or novel to externalize the creative inspiration resulting from different mediums (video games and literature) that were voicing the same story. For such a written reflection might have been a mere *sura* (form) that blinks but for a moment. But a connection that tethers a video game, play and scripture together is much more: a meaning that lingers, <u>foments</u>, then <u>ferments</u> into countless artistic images.

The artist is someone who must remain open, <u>silent</u> to <u>listen</u>, <u>expecting</u> the <u>exceptional</u>, and embracing the perplexity of being an in-between. This <u>consciously</u> <u>creative</u> human acknowledges that they, like everyone else, are a <u>waking</u> and <u>walking</u> imagination. The only thing distinguishing their forms as *jasad* (physical body), as opposed to *jism* (subtle corporeal image), is mere perception. With every <u>adventure</u> to our inner abyss, the hidden treasure, we <u>venture</u> into 'the land of reality'. There, we might sail across the ships of stone or see a galloping horse. Either way, it's enchanted and art.

Shariʿa of the Craft: On the Path to *Haqiqa*

"Poor is the pupil who does not surpass his master."
– Leonardo da Vinci

The architect Peter Cook refuses to use a computer to make blueprints of his designs. He <u>insists</u> on drawing by hand. When asked why he <u>persists</u> in this practice, he responds by saying: "I might be in the minority, but I believe that the struggle it takes my hands to master drawing something is just enough time for my mind to also comprehend it." This sage-artist has reached such a level of mastery in his craft that he is able to express his technique in universal lessons that apply to all disciplines.

The previous chapters have laid the metaphysical foundations of the creative process, through the lens of Sufis, specifically the writings of Ibn al-ʿArabi. This section and those that follow attempt to build a practical, yet still spiritual, vision of this framework that begins from the individual artist then expands to the society at large; one that needs to <u>thrive</u> and <u>survive</u> on its storytellers, artists, and myth weavers.

Our approach thus far has been to creatively overload the technical terms laden within the Islamic tradition. Phrases such as *haqiqa*, *'alam al-khayal*, *hayra*, and *maqam* have long since been imprisoned in the narrow box of theology. It is my objective in this book to liberate them and prove their <u>fecundity</u> as a <u>fertile</u> soil for a conversation about the spiritual dimensions of the creative process. Why, may you ask? Because, as I mentioned in the preface, I live by the conviction that the creative process and mystical experience are but <u>mere</u> <u>mirror</u> reflections of one another.

> *"The new meaning of soul is creativity and mysticism. These will become the foundation of the new psychological type and with him or her will come the new civilization."*
> – Otto Rank

In his groundbreaking work on Islamic history, *What is Islam: The Importance of Being Islamic*, Shahab Ahmed completely shifts the reader's perspective on how Islam, as a faith tradition, should be understood and approached. Instead of following the common – modernist – definition of religion as a 'system of beliefs and rituals', which the anthropologist Talal Asad has prudently described as a reflection of secularism and its invention, Ahmed instead describes Islam as a "process of making meaning."

This pays homage to Tweed's description of what religious women and men do, namely "making dwellings and crossing boundaries." But what Ahmed adds to this novel understanding of Islam is that neither the faith itself nor any of its constituent pillars and catechisms should be understood as static objects, but a toolset in a breadth of possible *bricolages*. This is the spirit in which we proceed in this book, looking at notions like *khayal* not only as imagination in an Islamic or Sufi sense, but as an idea, opening, and possibility.

To the abundant list of motifs that have accompanied us so far, we add three more terms to our conversation: *shari'a* (law/rules), *tariqa* (path), and *haqiqa* (reality). These are three central principles in Sufism, indicating the different phases of *suluk* (self-discipline) that a *murid* (disciple. Lit. desirer) goes through. Although we have discussed *suluk* in previous chapters, *murid* is a new term that requires our attention.

> *"Thoughts unspoken die unborn. The same goes for your paintings. If the desire lies within you, paint your heart out! But above all, keep developing because that's where real life begins."*
> – Tim Adams

Ibn al-'Arabi beautifully states in his litanies: "Oh God, I'm the *murad* [one desired] while you are the *murid* [one desiring]. So, make your *muradak* [desire] from me, such that you are the *murad* and I am the *murid*." A *murid* in Sufism is one who desires God and will go to the end of *maratib al-wujud* (the five levels of being) in order to reach their destination. In turn, God is the *murad* (object of desire) who is paradoxically present with the *murid* at every step of the journey. Rather, He is the *murid* seeking Himself.

If God and His creation are *murad* and *murid* respectively, then desire itself, also *murād* in Arabic, is none other than *al-haqiqa al-muhammadiyya* (the muhammadan reality) that we discussed in previous chapters. The primordial prophetic light is the life force that binds together all things in the universe, especially that which connects lover and beloved, and the artist with their craft. And here we bring these two terms, *murad* and *murid*, from theology and clothe in the garment of creativity to pay homage to both, the hidden treasure and seeking artist, respectively.

But just as God, the *murad*, is Himself the manifestation of His *murid*, so is the artist and their hidden treasure one and the same, but in different forms. This is but one of many roles that we play, as Shakespeare reiterates. Whether we journey into our inner abyss, still hoping to emerge sane, or leave our bodily flesh behind like Ghazali, we are ultimately actors who <u>play</u> and <u>pray</u> our parts in this cosmic dance.

"The desire to express myself can be triggered by any number of things — a particular experience, a childhood memory, a fleeting thought. Although these are often blurry, the images they evoke become sharper and clearer in time."
– Fernando Allevi

When John Lennon died, his friend and Beatles band member George Harrison was asked about his thoughts; his response simply was: "Oh you know, John took off one garment and put on another." Like Shakespeare and Ibn al-'Arabi, Harrison was a sage of his craft. He understood the universal movement at the heart of these uni-verse(s). He knew that at the peak of the mountain of creativity, one can also see the reflection at the summit of mysticism: they are one and the same.

Speaking of mountains, and their importance in the journeys of countless sages throughout human history, including the prophet ﷺ who received the first divine revelation while secluding himself in a cave atop a mountain overlooking Mecca, I once asked Sayyid Hossein Nasr, a prominent Sufi thinker about the importance that Ibn al-'Arabi has for the masses, since he is appreciated mostly by academics.

He said: "When people see a mountain, what attracts them is the peak. Only if the summit is beautiful enough will they go through the struggle to climb from the base." The siren song calls for the sage in religion, art, and every craft that demands mastery. When each arrives at the top, they can speak the same language, using the *nafis* (precious) meanings they inherited from their own technique, but clothing them in the tongue of universal humanity.

"Writing is magic, as much the water of life as any other creative art. The water is free. So, drink. Drink and be filled up."
– Stephen King

Mirroring the three terms *shari'a* (law/rules), *tariqa* (path), and *haqiqa* (reality) are also three types of faith that have been eloquently described by the 20th Malian Sufi sage Tierno Taal who compares these different phases to the three states of matter: *sulb* (solid), *sa'il* (liquid), and *ghazi* (gaseous). The first concerns the people of *taqlid* (imitation), whose faith "has a precise form; it is inflexible, hard like a rock. It is heavy and immobile like a mountain. If necessary, it prescribes armed warfare to assure its place and make it respected."

As for the second stage, the *sa'il* (liquid), it is one with "elements that flow from knowledge and are related to the truths from which they come, without one ever having to think about their origin or their existence from time immemorial." This can be considered an apt description for our journey in this book. Sufism, that proverbial water of knowledge is no longer solid in our eyes, and we can let it flow from its original container to a new one, creativity.

The people of the last stage, that of the *ghazi* (gaseous) faith, "are so pure that, released from all material weight that would hold them down on the earth, they rise like smoke into the heaven. Those who attain this faith worship God in truth and in a light beyond color." Bruce Lee, another sage of his craft, would agree with Tierno Taal. In the former's quote that we shared previously, he advised his listeners to "be like water." Meanwhile, the sage of Mali wants us to perceive a yet higher state of perception, the gaseous one, where no container can imprison the artist.

"If you must have a rule to follow, I would suggest cultivating a dialogue with your inner voice... If you listen to the clues your own images offer, the resulting work will be fresh, and authentic. Fall in love with your world."
– Jane Fulton Alt

Moreover, the concluding words of Taal, regarding those with the highest degree of faith, that they worship God in truth and in a light beyond color, is quite telling since hues behave differently in matter than light. In the first instance, the addition and subtraction of all colors results in black and white, respectively. In the second instance, the inverse is true. The addition and subtraction of all colors in light results in white and black, respectively. In other words, our *nasut* and *lahut* are mere reflective mirrors of one another. Our physical form, with all its eccentricities, allows us to appreciate our spiritual dispositions.

With this understanding of the three states of faith, we return to the three pillars of Sufism with which we began this chapter: *shari'a* (law/rules), *tariqa* (path), and *haqiqa* (reality). The first of these is a widespread term in our day and age that has been abused well into controversy. Whether it is punishment laws, oppression of women, or forced conversions to Islam, *shari'a* is a term that has become synonymous with everything that many people hate about this beautiful faith.

It is a heartbreaking circumstance that the rules of the craft of *suluk* (self-discipline) should be so abused and, in turn, misunderstood. This is all the more reason for us to view *shari'a* in this book from another vantage point: art and creativity. I will not linger on the legalistic dimension of the 'law' in Islam, only to highlight that Ibn al-'Arabi dedicates about 800 pages of his magnum opus, *The Meccan Openings*, to the inner spiritual dimensions of *shari'a*.

> *"Learn the rules in drawing and perspective. It is an absolute must, even for the abstract artist, to learn the rules before perfecting a personal style."*
> – William Band

It is here that we find some of the Sufi mystic's most innovative discussions, where he lets the reader know that *malakut* (spiritual realm) and *nasut* (physical world) are on an absolute continuum, communicating through the realm of *jabarut*, otherwise known as *'alam al-khayal* (imagination). He begins from the laws governing the body and perceives its wisdom in the way of the spirit, just as he explains the reason behind the necessity of performing the ritual wash using running, not still water because movement is life.

Other examples here include his explanation for the permissibility of wearing footwear during *salat* (prayer). Unconcerned with worldly causes, he states instead that prayer is a journey, and one cannot travel barefoot. As we have discussed earlier, prayer is actually an ascension, whereby *sujud* (prostration) is the symbolic mountain peak where one enters the divine presence of *lahut* (divinity). Hence, as we stated, the prophet's ﷺ statement that "the entire earth has been designated as a *masjid* [place of prostration]" is an expansive invitation to perceive everyone and everything around us as a manifestation of our hidden treasure.

Perhaps the Sufi mystic would also like us to perceive the rules of any craft not as mere <u>constrictions</u> but <u>constructions</u> that allow us to climb, <u>hear</u>, and listen to the siren song at the summit of our inner mountain, <u>here</u> and now. As Sayyid Hossein Nasr stated, it is that peak that attracts climbers towards the awe-inspiring silent vision atop the <u>world</u>, <u>word</u>, and language. But as the painter William Band told us, even the most abstract peak requires a sturdy base, and herein lies the importance of rules: a bodily <u>prayer</u> preluding spiritual <u>play</u>.

> *"There are rules in drawing that cannot be broken. It is math. But the rules can be bent, and new rules invented."*
> – Moncy Barbour

There is no art form or craft that lacks a *shari'a*. The way a painter holds a brush, a musician plays scales, or a poet understands the grammar of their medium are all rules of the trade. However, as Ibn al-'Arabi and all artists show us, imprisoning and reducing a craft to its laws is akin to destroying a beautiful mountain down to its base, where it cannot even be seen from afar. The rules let us <u>read</u> the <u>road</u> and <u>tread</u> it; they sacrifice themselves into *khumul* (dormancy).

This is a symbolism built into the term *shari'a* itself. The word is a derivative of *shari'* (road). In pre-Islamic times, the word *shari'a* was used by Arabs to indicate the path to water, itself a very rare and *nafis* (precious) commodity in the Arabian desert. In turn, Islam came and paid homage to this cultural usage by emphasizing that the rules of *suluk* (self-discipline) ought to be appreciated as a necessary path to the water of life, domain of the spirit, and hidden treasure.

And many of the problems in religion – and other crafts – arise when the path is confused with destination, when the rules are worshipped instead of divinity. Here, the works of the sages of art have much to teach us. When I first began to reflect on the topic of this chapter, I was struck by the simple fact that no one ever desires to become a painter by watching Picasso practice the rules of holding his brush, a musician by listening to Beethoven practice chords, or a poet by reading Hemingway's high school grammar homework.

> *"Learn the rules like an amateur, then break them like an pro."*
> – Pablo Picasso

On the contrary, it is the visions these sages have translated from their inner *lahut* that have stopped us in our tracks. We hear the story of existence, all five levels of being, in Beethoven's *Moonlight Sonata*. We taste suffering and redemption in the empty spaces between Hemingway's words, much less the actual ink of his letters. We perceive the primordial divine colors in Picasso's paintings. All the while, we are peeking into law, path, and all reality from the peak of a unitary vision.

And so, learning one or a thousand rules of your craft means only one thing: you still have to take the path. The Jordanian musician Tariq al-Jundi, a sage of his craft, states that learning the rules of Arabic music is akin to someone learning Arabic grammar, which in no way means they have become poets. The difference between two people who stand in front of a crowd and say: "Welcome ladies and gentlemen", the first without intonation or emotion while the second much more poetically, makes all the difference in the <u>world</u> and <u>word</u>. This is despite the fact that, in both instances, the grammar is correct.

Transitioning to *tariqa*, the path, this is the arduous climb up the mountain of craft and – more importantly – self-discovery. Martin Broadwell, a management trainer, developed a four-stage model of competence that harmonizes with our discussion here. The first step, 'unconsciously incompetent', refers to our unawareness of the inability to perform or master a craft. Before learning the oud, I watched virtuosos play the instrument and thought it easy. Not only did I lack the knowledge to play the oud but was also unaware of my ignorance.

> *"Learn the rules, and then forget them."*
> – Matsuo Basho

Then, when one takes the path, they become 'consciously incompetent' and gain awareness of their weaknesses and shortcomings. Here, it is not enough to simply know our inability to play a musical instrument, draw a shape, or apply poetic meters. Rather, *'ubur* (crossing over) is paramount, from the metaphor of the craft back into our inner *lahut* to <u>see</u> what our art <u>seeks</u> to tell us about ourselves. Perhaps my inability to solemnly hold the oud in my lap is an allegory for my fragility in embracing certain aspects about myself: these keep sliding away from me without making music that is pleasant to the ear.

Next, comes the stage of 'consciously competent', where we begin to chisel away at our weaknesses in the craft, all the while introspectively <u>healing</u> our inner wounds and deciphering our Achilles <u>heel</u>. Despite the fact that this phase seems to be the height of mastery, where competence finally emerges, it is still not the summit of our journey. That peak is reserved for those who become 'unconsciously competent'. This is when your art is a conversation between your pick and the guitar, pen and paper, brush and canvas, while you silently observe. You become nothing; hence everything can be channeled through you.

"Creativity requires faith. Faith requires that we relinquish control."
– Julia Cameron, *The Artist's Way*

In his master class on acting, Sir Michael Caine mentions a story about Jack Lemon's first time in front of the camera. Coming from a theater background, Lemon was used to projecting and magnifying his voice in order that his performance reaches the audience. However, film requires the opposite: a lessening of movements since the <u>lens</u> can easily pick up every <u>sense</u>, both apparent and hidden.

In one scene, the director repeatedly asks Lemon: "Do less Jack!" After many takes, the actor responded: "If I do any less, I'll do nothing." To which the director replied: "Now you've got it Jack!" Doing and being nothing is of the essence for the sage. As God lovingly addresses His prophet ﷺ: "You have no hand in the affair" (3:128). This statement has often been misinterpreted as belittling the prophet's role. In reality, however, it is a testimony to the immense love and care that God has for him: "Do not do anything, for I will take care of all your affairs!"

The *wali* (sage) in any craft is described beautifully in one of the prophet's teachings, explaining that God loves nothing more than to be approached through those things that He has made obligatory. Meanwhile, the person continues to draw nearer to Him through optional worship until He loves them. When He loves them, He becomes the sight with which they see, the hearing with which they hear, the hand with which they work and foot with which they march.

It should not be understood from this that, prior to worship, God does not love human beings. For what are talents, beauty, and the facilitation to cultivate our hidden treasure anything but signs of His love? Rather, it is through our struggle to climb that mountain, to learn and apply the *shari'a* of our craft carefully that the extent of this love is truly unveiled for us. Prior to all of this, we might feel as though we are living in a continuous and unrelenting creative block.

> *"Creativity requires the courage to let go of certainties."*
> – Erich Fromm

In her groundbreaking work on creativity, *The Artist's Way*, Julia Cameron sets the frontier to help us perceive this mirroring effect between craft and life. Building on her quote from the previous page, the author reiterates that "the creative process is a process of surrender, not control." This is a lesson about life, not only art. We have already deciphered this much from the architect Peter Cook who refuses to draw blueprints save by hand. It goes without saying that Cameron's gift inspired the impetus for this book.

What the *Artist's Way* also gives us is the ability to <u>reframe</u> and <u>re-form</u> key spiritual stations, such as *shukr* (gratitude) that we discussed above, in terms of the journey of the artist and creative process. One of the thresholds that I hope this book opens is a deeper conversation about all the spiritual *maqamat* (stations) in *suluk* (self-discipline), including the rituals of *shariʿa* (e.g., *salat* (prayer), *wudu* (ablution), *zakat* (alms)) and what these terms mean in the world of the artist. This is the method, I believe, in which Islam generally and Sufism specifically may become – as Shahab Ahmed had hoped – a 'process of making meaning' for creative souls everywhere.

> *"With every stitch, I became art. Beautifully broken. But still standing."*
> – Debra Pry

As an example, I would like to offer my own reflection here about *tawba* (repentance), the first *maqam* (spiritual station) in *suluk* and its place in an artist's life. Recently, I watched an interview with South African photographer Mikhael Subotzky who has the peculiar practice of intentionally cracking the glass frame embracing his photographs. The reason is that he would like his audience to see his work as not reality and also guide them to other aspects of an image, such as texture, color, or light, all of which are dimensions that are unveiled for us once the <u>heart</u> acknowledges that it is looking at <u>art</u>.

Watching this interview, I immediately remembered the beautiful Japanese art of *kintsugi*, where broken pottery is repaired by attaching the pieces together using powdered gold. The shattered glass that reveals the art of a photograph, broken pottery that is beautified by gold, and the repentant heart of a human being returning to divinity in brokenness became a singular *maʿna* (meaning) for me, one that appears in many possible *suwar* (forms).

If Subotzky's work and *kintsugi* gave me an artistic insight into the reality of *tawba*, then I need to repay art for this gift and decipher what repentance actually means for the artist. It is the return, devotion, and unwavering <u>commitment</u> to <u>communicate</u> with your hidden treasure, especially after neglecting and forgetting that inner *lahut* (divinity). The repentance of the artist is coming with a humbled and broken, yet golden and beautiful, <u>heart</u> to their <u>art</u>.

> *"A teacher affects eternity. He can never tell where his influence stops."*
> – Henry Adams

Another photographer, Richard Misrach, has already shown us the reality of *salat* (prayer) for the artist. As the prophet ﷺ turned away from his surroundings when prayer called to him, so should the artist, as Misrach does, also become oblivious to everything when a scene is ready to be born through their eyes. Likewise, *zakat* (alms) of the artist is the charity due to the world. It need not be an actual work of art, but simply a small Christic miracle that they cast on a dead *nafs* (soul); one that longs for the *nafas* (breath) of creativity.

Lastly, concerning one of the five main pillars of Islam, *hajj* (pilgrimage), I would like to recount another series of connections that manifested almost a decade ago. In 2010, I visited The Art Institute of Chicago's Museum where there was a temporary <u>exhibit</u> of works by the early 20th century painter Henri Matisse. Hidden in this <u>exquisite</u> display was a large biographical book in which I found a conversation between Matisse and one of his students.

The disciple and teacher were in a philosophical disagreement about drawing objects from the world. Matisse believed that an artist should sit and <u>silently</u> observe the given object they wish to draw, <u>listening</u> attentively until it gives them what it wishes to convey. On the other hand, the student believed that a painter has complete control over the subject of their work and should have the freedom to interpret the narrative in any shape they desire. This debate continued until Matisse sensed that his student simply wanted to disagree and prove his worth as an independent artist.

At this point, Matisse gives his student, what could very well be considered, a Sufi sage's advice to their *murid* (disciple/seeker). Quoting Cézanne, Matisse states that every beginning artist needs to visit the Louvre and try to find their *murad* (sage/sought after) in the works on display. Once the spirit of a sage speaks to the student, from behind the vale, the latter need to devote their lives to bringing the master's vision to life.

> *"So do these wonders a most dizzy pain,*
> *That mingles Grecian grandeur with the rude*
> *Wasting of old time—with a billowy main—*
> *A sun—a shadow of a magnitude."*
> – John Keats, *On Seeing the Elgin Marbles*

This remarkable exchange reminded me of a book my mother had been reading at the time, *The Mona Lisa Strategem* by Harriet Rubin. She recounted to me one excerpt that had caught her attention. It discussed the final moments in Da Vinci's life, during which he was embracing his painting. When he breathed his last, the guards at the door went to peel the work from his body's embrace. The king stopped and commanded them to leave the Mona Lisa for a while until Da Vinci's spirit completely permeates the painting.

An image of the <u>museum</u> as a <u>mausoleum</u> was emerging clearly in my mind and heart, yet there was one final piece of the puzzle that further cemented this vision. In *Rethinking Islamic Studies*, contributor Louis Ruprecht gives an eye-opening account of the birth of the modern museum. Constructed as an imagined space where citizens of newly founded nation states in modernity can go to negotiate and discover their identities, the museum was – essentially – a pilgrimage <u>site</u> and <u>sight</u>. It is a place where <u>memories</u> are simultaneously <u>remembered</u> and constructed. Ruprecht mentions two poets, John Keats and Lord Byron who visited aging artifacts of the old world and considered these journeys as pilgrimages that transform both, body and spirit.

"If a part of night is inscribed in language, this is also language's moment of effacement. This nocturnal side of speech could be called obsession. A forger can imitate a painter's brush stroke or a writer's style and make the difference between them imperceptible, but he will never be able to make his own their obsession, what forces them to be always going back toward that silence where the first imprints are sealed."
– Anne Dufourmantelle, *Of Hospitality*

The last connection in this play of pilgrimage is the French philosopher Jacques Derrida's *Of Hospitality* and its interweaved brilliant commentary by Anne Dufourmantelle. Amidst the poetic exchange that animates the pages of this work, Derrida speaks about *l'étranger* (the foreigner) from *l'étranger* (abroad): those who cannot find their identity in the soil of birth and so, must await the moment of death to know where they truly belonged.

The anthropologist Engseng Ho would agree with Derrida. In his work *Graves of Tarim* he discusses the itineraries of *sayyids* (descendants of the prophet ﷺ) in India and Indonesia whose ancestors had traveled from far away Yemen, intermarried in these places, and spread the message of Islam there. Many centuries later, their offspring retrace their steps back to the shrines of their forefathers in the holy city of Tarim, Yemen as a means of knowing the self.

Ibn al-ʿArabi says in one of his poems that "In ʿArafat I have *ʿaraftu* [come to know] the One you desire." ʿArafat is the name of the mount surrounding Mecca where pilgrims stand to perform their most important rite during the season of *hajj*: to climb the peak, supplicate, and hope to hear the siren song calling back from heaven. Incidentally – or perhaps co-incidentally – the name ʿArafat is a derivative of *maʿrifa* (gnosis), hence the Sufi mystic <u>perceived</u> standing on this hilltop as a metaphor for <u>receiving</u> direct inner knowledge of God, divinity, and the hidden treasure.

> *"Begin by learning to draw and paint like the old masters. After that, you can do as you like; everyone will respect you."*
> – Salvador Dali

Pilgrimage for the artist is the journey to find the sage of their craft, one whose only qualification is that they have mastered and treaded the mountain all the way to the peak. They are those who can teach you about the <u>craft</u> and how to sail the <u>raft</u> of life. They need not be of your religion or ethnicity, but only that they hear God speak through their pen, brush, pick, or camera lens, even if they are atheist. It is their prerogative to call their hidden treasure flow or *lahut*, while it is your duty to drink their wisdom in your cup.

These sages of the craft are the ones who have reached the *haqiqa* (reality) of their art. Whereas the beginners, still learning the *shariʿa* (rules) of their passion, may only be able to think in solid terms, judging musical notes to be wrong or certain meetings between colors to be incorrect. Meanwhile, those who tread the *tariqa* (path) are constantly humbled. They begin to hear the <u>whispers</u> and <u>wisdoms</u> emanating from their instrument everywhere, like liquid water moving smoothly between containers.

Sages like Matisse, Picasso, Coltrane, Al Pacino, Spielberg, Hemingway, and Shakespeare have ascended the mountain. They speak in a universal language. They see both, water and cup, <u>craft</u> and <u>raft</u> in a singular vision. These are the artists who have become art. Somedays, when the poem I hope to write does not want to engage with me, I will seek the sages from my motherland, such as Khalil Gibran, Naguib Mahfouz, Nizar Kabbani, or Mahmoud Darwish to voice <u>one</u> through me. <u>One</u> of them always answers.

"You can waste your lives drawing lines. Or you can live your life crossing them."
– Shonda Rhimes

Once we begin to perceive Islam and Sufism as a 'process of making meaning', as Shahab Ahmed had suggested, we begin to appreciate the Malian sage Tierno Taal's three-tiered differentiation of faith as solid, liquid, and gas. A bit of a confession: for a long time, I had wondered how best to describe my inclination to 'make connections where none seem possible or exist', one of the two definitions of creativity that I have stated in the preface of this book.

It was not until I came across Taal's framework that my eccentric inclination to translate the very technical, legalistic, and theological contours of my faith into the realm of creativity made perfect sense. It is not by choice that I constantly make these crossings between <u>crafts</u>, using the <u>raft</u> of my imagination. Rather, this is part of my disposition as a first-generation Arab Muslim immigrant, born to a family of artists, whose spirituality was <u>founded</u> in America, and I continue to <u>find</u> the summit of my faith best represented in contemporary Western Art and culture.

I will not make claims as to whether my faith has surpassed the solid state. I believe that becoming infatuated by this, even if I happen to reside at the highest peak of gaseous *iman* (faith), is an <u>obsession</u> that will become a <u>possession</u>; and such an empty <u>arrogance</u> is itself <u>ignorance</u> and a solid state of <u>contention,</u> under the false guise of <u>contentment</u>. Instead, to use Ibn al-ʿArabi's definition of love, I would like us to appreciate the journey, the constant movement and translation between what our minds seek to separate but our <u>heart</u> longs to <u>hear</u> and host in a conversation.

That migration between different abodes is for me the essence of creativity. A poem, painting, or piece of music is a photograph of one's creative state. Like a star that has moved on eons ago, yet we are still able to enjoy its light. Likewise, a work of art is a lingering glimmer of the dive into that abyss of our hidden treasure. Where the artist is now, and where they will be in the future, has to be heard in the silence of music, stillness of color, and emptiness of ink. Like the artist-sages of *haqiqa* (reality), one can best perform what they have mastered only by being and doing nothing.

What words cannot describe,
Colors can prescribe.
And what hues cannot perceive,
Music may very well receive.

I have <u>adopted</u> and <u>adapted</u> the above from Inayat Khan's *Mysticism of Sound and Music.*

Following these traces, the next set of chapters will delve into the written, visual, auditory, and moving arts respectively.

Memories in Ink: On the Written Arts

"Write quickly and you will never write well; write well, and you will soon write quickly."
– Marcus Fabius Quintilianus

I like to think of writing as my native creative language. I began voicing my thoughts on paper serendipitously after I began reading the works of Ibn al-ʿArabi in the summer of 2012 while applying for a graduate program in Islamic studies. It is a testimony to the *hayra* (perplexity) of creativity and how it is born, behooving the artist to always <u>expect</u> the <u>exceptional</u>, that I was born a writer when my intention was otherwise, to become an academic.

I owe you, the reader, a reason as to why I pursued a PhD in Islamic Studies in the first place. As I stated in the previous chapter, I am a first-generation Arab Muslim immigrant who found his faith in America; the same country whose warplanes had bombed my place of birth, Iraq in 1990 thereby forcing my family and I to begin a life of migration and diaspora. That was the first in a series of paradoxes that would color my life: finding my faith in a country whose military tentacles sought to destroy me. But such is the life of the artist: our suffering is the ink, color, and sound with which we redeem ourselves.

I had already mentioned the details of my 'rebirth' in the preface, but I shall reiterate the essential scenes here. In 2012, after completing my masters in Artificial Intelligence two years prior, I sought the humanities for two reasons: to better understand the meaning of intelligence in human beings and be accepted by a religious community that would not accept anybody's opinion about their faith without a degree in Islamic studies, even if they are practicing Muslims.

> *"All creative people want to do the unexpected."*
> – Hedy Lamarr

Also as mentioned in the preface, little did I know that the only thing worse than not having any degree in Islamic Studies is obtaining an academic education without its classical counterpart at a seminary. I sought to be accepted by people and was promptly sent away. And like many who are rejected at every turn, <u>art</u> embraced me with open <u>arms</u>. The massive amount of pages that I read during the summer of 2012, both from Ibn al-'Arabi's own books, other Sufi mystics, and secondary references in English were incessant knocks on the gate of my hidden treasure to awaken.

And it did with a beautiful vengeance. This began with a longing in Arabic in the form of written reflections on the Sufi mystic that I composed in my native tongue. Of course, his own teachings and dancing with this language via an innovative etymology was rewiring my heart and allowing me to think abstractly about language. More importantly, I started to perceive myself as a host between these two guests, Arabic and English, in a conversation across time and space.

Herein lies the most rewarding gift I have received, not only from Ibn al-ʿArabi, but also my hidden treasure and the metacosmic *lahut*: translation itself is a true art. In my various self-published collections of poetic reflections, titled *Art in Memoirs* volumes one and two, the spirit of the work remains in what is truly unsaid; that movement back and forth between each reflection's Arabic and English mirrors. How can I render eloquence from one language to a new clothing in an entirely new register?

> *"The original is unfaithful to the translation."*
> – Jorge Luis Borges

I usually never retort to literal translations and actually abhor this practice when used in the transformation of *qasidas* (religious odes) from Arabic to English. For how the Arab <u>ear</u> understands eloquence and the English <u>hears</u> it are entirely different. They are processes that are conceived, birthed, and mature in culture. This is why, for quite some time now, I have found the lyrics of John Denver, Bob Dylan, Adele, and the Beatles to be a more harmonious form of Sufi poetry in contemporary America than a literally translated *qasida* that, despite its sacredness in Arabic, is able to neither <u>carry</u> nor <u>convey</u> its original spark in a new tongue.

And why should the poetry of Dylan, Frost, or Keats not be assumed to be the spiritual imprint of our day, age, and place? In his foreword to Henry

Corbin's *Alone with the Alone: Creative Imagination in the Sufism of Ibn Arabi*, Harold Bloom states that divine imagination can be perceived easier today in the words of Shakespeare than Ibn al-'Arabi. While I agree in principle with Bloom, I think much of our perspective changes once we think of the Sufi mystic's teachings as a 'process of making meaning' that embraces all contexts, from Arabic to English and all that is in-between.

This is ultimately what translation is all about: rising as a writer from the level of content to <u>context</u>, without which you <u>con</u> the <u>text</u>. This is a return to Taal's gaseous faith and the artist-sages of *haqiqa* who stand at the summit with a unitary vision. They view all of human creativity as a singular *ma'na* (meaning) that emerges continuously in new *suwar* (forms). It is a recurring archetype, from religion to writing and life: a solid state of faith <u>constricts</u> and <u>restricts</u>, whereas a liquid or gaseous conviction keeps us moving, <u>constructing</u> and <u>assisting</u>.

> *"We've got truth and lies and then there's this little space, the edge, in the middle.*
> *That liminal space, that's art."*
> – Mac Barnett

Each of the words in Arabic and English that bring life to my poetry have memories associated with them. Sometimes these come as smells, tastes, colors, scenes, or sounds. As I mentioned in the preface, a childhood orphaned of a motherland is the source of all my creative inspiration. It is a hidden treasure that has been dormant for decades, slowly accumulating its constituent parts and waiting for the right moment to awaken, much like the muhammadan reality that manifests gradually through prophets and sages over the course of humanity. And so it is that this childhood in exile is my very own light of the prophet ﷺ that keeps breathing. For whatever results in beauty – even in the form of suffering – must necessarily be from that source.

I have also realized that my desire to write a poem in both Arabic and English, side by side, is a subconscious attempt to reenact and embody my own bodily migration(s) on ink and paper. I can retrace each of my steps across the sands of Iraq and Jordan or soaring above the sea on my way to America within the curvature of every letter. Meanwhile, the silence between the words hearkens for those moments of perplexity when my awareness of being in the *barzakh* (in-between) was vivid.

> *"A reader lives a thousand lives before he dies . . . The man who never reads lives only one."*
> – George R.R. Martin

I often advise readers of my books who do not know Arabic to try and read the calligraphy of the letters. If your <u>mind</u> cannot <u>mind</u> the grammar of a language, then let your <u>heart</u> <u>hear</u> its curvature instead. It is a heightened state of awareness to <u>read</u> the <u>reed</u> of a language at such a primordial level, liberated from the <u>expectations</u> of grammar and awaiting *l'avenir*, that looming and <u>unexpected</u> hidden treasure, to make itself known.

I have used this same advice in my retreats when instructing fellow Muslims on how to approach the Qur'an; to imagine how different our perception of divine communication would be if we enjoyed it as we do a painting by Picasso, Monet, or Matisse at a museum. As soon as we enter this modern mausoleum of artist-sage shrines, an entirely different set of faculties are activated within us. We recognize the sacred presence, one that reminds us of an ancient age where the <u>play</u> of art was our <u>prayer</u>.

We do not look at a painting to criticize the shade of colors, perfection of drawn lines, or the meeting between characters on canvas. Often, the guiding question within is: "What does this work say to us? How does it speak to our inner voice?" Our world – yes, the entire earth – would be a much better place if we all read our external and internal scriptures this way. More than that, if we were to perceive all manifestations of a hidden treasure as an entextment of the *kitab marqum* (cryptic book, the human being), it would truly be a three-tiered transformation in microcosm, macrocosm, and metacosm.

"In the case of good books, the point is not to see how many of them you can get through, but rather how many can get through to you."
– Mortimer Adler

A book is also more than its words. Like Subotzky's wise strategy of shattering the glass frame embracing his photographs, we need to <u>shatter</u> our obsession with content and <u>shudder</u> more at the <u>memories</u> that are imprinted as <u>remembrance</u> in the margins: within the wrinkled paper, binding, cover choice, forewords, and prefaces that ornament the story with its first breath. That is the silence before the plunge. All the countless drafts that an author has surreptitiously tried to efface from the final version are still there. They whisper like an omen from the beyond. As Elbert Hubbard eloquently put it: "Grammar is the grave of letters."

And so, nowadays we have countless books on the subject of 'how to read a book'. But we never seek to know how to read the <u>foreboding body</u> of a book. Not only the sandy shore from cover to the first wave of content, but also that calligraphy that we alluded to above. It is a self-standing art to distinguish between the personality of each word, or even letter, and how it seeks to establish its unique presence. No two instances of A, B, or C are the same. As Ibn al-'Arabi has told us: there is no 'repetition in creation'.

"An Arabic expression is like the oud, if you strike one of its strings, all others will ring for you and vibrate. Then, the language will stir inside the soul, beyond the immediate meaning, an entourage of emotions and images."
– William Marçais

The Moroccan Sufi saint 'Abdul 'Aziz al-Dabbagh teaches that although the Qur'an contains the same Arabic letters found in words that are not part of scripture, those in the former are not the same as their counterparts in normal speech; they contain altogether different lights. One of al-Dabbagh's miracles was his ability to see a different glow emanating from a speaker's mouth if they were uttering a verse, teaching of the prophet ﷺ, statement by a scholar or a non-religious expression in Arabic.

The Sufi sage even goes as far as saying that the word *bab* (door), for example, which is found in the Qur'an has an altogether different reality than when an Arab utters it referring to the door in their house. Using the same analogy, all writers in a given language use the same alphabet, but how distinct are their lights and energies. They emanate from a different heart, hidden treasure and inner *lahut*. And with each author who clothes the organs of their language with a new dress of metaphor and meaning, it is all the better for that tongue. It continues to live.

For Ibn al-ʿArabi, all aspects of human culture, including language, are sacred and rooted in divinity. In the case of Arabic specifically, this is vividly visible in the fact that the Qurʾan, as God's literal speech, came in the tongue of the Arabs. But all languages, ultimately, have a sacred origin. However, as al-Dabbagh also states, many of the world's languages have lost the trace of their original childhood, whereas Arabic remains, due to the Qurʾan, a remnant of that ancient source.

"The mediocre teacher tells. The good teacher explains. The superior teacher demonstrates. The great teacher inspires."
– William Arthur Ward

But let us not forget that Shahab Ahmed has already advised not to consider Islam, the Arabic language included, as a static object but rather a 'process of making meaning'. Such a shift in perspective allows us to perceive the tongue of the Qurʾan as a medium through which other registers may remember and unlock their sacred origins as well. Moreover, this is a task not exclusive to Arabic, but other European languages, such as French or Latin, can also fulfill this mission.

However, I speak from my experience as a native speaker of Arabic, who happens to write poetry in both this language and English; when I contemplate my thoughts in the first register and write in the second, altogether different pathways are forged in the tongue of Shakespeare, Hemingway, and Frost. The countless instances of underlined terms throughout this book, meant to highlight anagrams, homonyms, contranyms, or alliterations are nothing but an homage to the way Arabic has made me appreciate the magic of English.

But lest I myself forget, it was Ibn al-ʿArabi who helped me decipher Arabic and the highest manifestation of its eloquence, the Qurʾan, in new ways. This series of mediations is neither unique to me nor the Arabic language. As I mentioned in a previous chapter, every beginning artist who has sought to climb the mountain of their craft was necessarily attracted and moved to do so by witnessing a work of *haqiqa* (reality) produced by a sage who sits at that peak.

"Somewhere in my head, a private conviction exists that 'Search is the Process' and 'Discovery the Art Form."
– Abe Ajay

In *Kafka on the Shore*, Haruki Murakami ends his metaphysically-rich fictional journey through his native Japan with a beautiful scene involving a thick forest. The protagonist enters these woods, while in the physical world, only to find himself exiting from the other side in purgatory or some kind of spiritual realm where he interacts with the dead. For me, this image greatly symbolizes the Sacred and how it makes itself appear in Arabic. For you can have novels and stories that are thoroughly mired in the mundane, between coffee, food, childhood, and neighborhood fights. At the far end of the spectrum, there are litanies that contain names of angels and spirits unknown to man, all using the same alphabet.

Again, this is just one of the many ways in which Arabic, as part of a process known as Islam or Sufism, can help us rekindle our enchantment in language, as an ideal. Who says that the words of Shakespeare, Frost or lyrics of Dylan and John Denver cannot be shaman dances that <u>stir</u> the heavens or <u>split</u> the earth asunder? But it is never a matter of what the words themselves can or cannot do, only the power with which we infuse them and then – hopefully – release them with breaths that carry an equal amount of conviction.

"He who knows no foreign languages knows nothing of his own."
– Johann Wolfgang von Goethe

Before transitioning to a more metaphysical conversation on the sacredness of language, I would like to give an example of how the art of translation manifests in my own creative process. I recently came across this well-known Arab proverb that demonstrates the eloquence of the language. I write it here in its original – for those who might want to read the calligraphy – and its transliteration to appreciate the effects of rhyming homonyms. Then, I will discuss my own process of rendering this in English, such that it can continue to maintain its original spirit, despite the drastic change in garb.

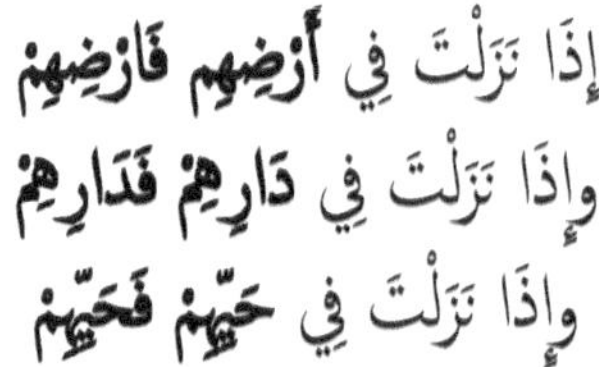

Idhā nazalta fī <u>arḍihim</u> <u>fa-arḍihim</u>
Wa idhā nazalta fī <u>dārihim</u> <u>fa-dārihim</u>
Wa idhā nazalta fī <u>ḥayyihim</u> <u>fa-ḥayyihim</u>

If I had resorted to a literal translation of these verses, the following would have been the rather dead result:

> If you come to **their land**, then **make them happy**
> And if you come to **their house**, then **take care of them**
> And if you come to **their neighborhood**, then **greet them**

Given that the movement of this Arabic proverb resides less so in the actual meaning of words and more in a phonetic dance and rhyming homonyms, my objective in composing an English translation should remain true to this spirit, in a manner that is equally loyal to the new register's own standards of eloquence. With all this in mind, this is the English portrait I painted for this expression:

> If you **land** in their **land**, then **hand** them a **hand**
> And if you **board** their **abode**, then **bode** a well **ode**
> And if you **align** with their **alley**, then be a **light** and **ally lightly**

This is hardly a literal translation of the Arabic. However, it certainly is – I feel – closer to it in spirit. What I focused on was not meaning but the structures of language that the Arabs had utilized in their *bricolage*; then, I tried to find the same arsenal available to me in English. Whereas in the Arabic all three lines rely on homonyms that have the same pronunciation, the English portrait utilizes this form only in the first verse, while in the second and third it resorts heavily to rhyming <u>endings</u> and <u>bindings</u>.

> *"Let me live, love, and say it well in good sentences."*
> – Sylvia Plath, *The Unabridged Journals of Sylvia Plath*

An excursion into the metaphysics of language takes us back to Ibn al-'Arabi's vision of Jesus, particularly his description in the Qur'an as the 'Word of God' and the characterization of Mary as one who 'believed in the Words of her Lord', both of which were discussed in the first chapter. The Sufi mystic takes these two verses into account when he says that the words which Christ's mother believed in were none other than Jesus himself.

This is because the son of Mary can be considered a single word in his entirety, but also each of his parts is an utterance. Naturally, this means that every human being is also a word of God, and each of our parts (i.e., bodily, psychological, spiritual) are an utterance as well. In other places in *The Meccan Openings*, the author describes each of the organs and dimensions of the human being as letters that come together to form a sacred word.

> *"You must stay drunk on writing so reality cannot destroy you."*
> – Ray Bradbury, *Zen in the Art of Writing*

Ibn al-ʿArabi also distinguishes between divine speech and words. When Moses comes to speak with God at Mount Sinai, the Qurʾan describes their exchange as one of speech. Upon hearing God speak, the prophet of the Israelites fainted. Hence, the Sufi mystic states that had He spoke with Mary as He did with Moses, she would have fainted as well. Rather, He only cast a single word upon her, that being Jesus. Here, the author is voicing his opinion about a centuries-long debate regarding the eternality of divine speech and whether the Qurʾan is created or uncreated.

However, like us, he is not so much interested in dialectics. Rather, he unfurls the universality of this distinction, between divine *kalam* (speech) and *kalimat* (words), to say that all of creation are "God's words that do not expire." Whereas *kalam* is eternal, *kalimat* (sg. *kalima*) are incessantly created, yet exist only momentarily before perishing, since – you guessed it! – there can be no repetition in creation.

As we mentioned in chapter one, *On Storytelling*, the terms *kalam*, *kalima*, and *kalimat* are all siblings of *kalim* (wound), whence Ibn al-ʿArabi has drawn the beautiful analogy of the words of God imprinting themselves upon the empty canvas of existence, just as pen wounds paper. In this sense, we stated, the Sufi mystic believes in a spiritual crucifixion that is none other than Christ himself, for the latter is the <u>word</u> of God that had first imprinted itself in Mary's <u>womb</u> and later in the <u>world</u> through Jesus' miracle performance.

> *"We write to taste life twice, in the moment and in retrospect."*
> – Anaïs Nin

What we did not discuss in that chapter, however, is that Ibn al-ʿArabi speaks extensively in the beginning of *The Meccan Openings* about *ʿilm al-huruf* (the science of letters). This is a hermetic knowledge that can be found in the writings of Greek philosophers and even earlier civilizations. It is an ancient discipline that was tethered to others, such as numerology and astrology. One can find its presence today in many Sufi writings and other spiritual traditions in litanies that call upon spiritual beings by referencing names that reside beyond human language yet can still be uttered in the Arabic alphabet.

After describing the technicalities of numerology and the specific spiritual powers that are assigned to each of the letters in Arabic, Ibn al-ʿArabi once again reaches the shore of universality and tells us that letters in a language are nations and tribes like human beings. Each of them has a character and personality that differs from others. They may even be considered to have children, and receive a divine calling through messengers, just like us.

The Sufi mystic beautifully compares the creation of the human being to a word because they are both essentially one and the same. Just as the human bodily composition consists of the four elements: water, earth, fire, and air, so are words composed of letters, the elements of language. Moreover, just as God breathes life into the human form, so does the skeleton of words also receive the spark of meaning through _harakat_ (accents) in Arabic that _tuharrik_ (move) the letters into being.

It should not be surprising as to why Ibn al-ʿArabi believes that _taʿbir_ (interpretation) and _ʿubur_ (crossing over) are processes that not only apply to _al-kitab al-mastur_ (written book) but also _al-kitab al-marqum_ (ciphered book, microcosm) and _al-kitab al-manzur_ (witnessed book, macrocosm). The Sufi mystic takes to heart the status of the cosmos, human being included, as words of God and hopes that we engage with our surroundings just as we would reading a book.

"Writers and artists know that ethereal moment, when just one, fleeting something—a chill, an echo, the click of a lamp, a question—ignites the flame of an entire work that blazes suddenly into consciousness."
– Nadine C. Keels

We have spoken about the importance of not only deciphering the content of a book, but also its body, otherwise known as context. Similarly, Ibn al-ʿArabi would like us to read both, the content of the cosmos – its macrocosmic _nasut_ (physical world) – as well as its context: the realms of _jabarut_ (imagination), _malakut_ (spiritual kingdom), and _lahut_ (divinity). It is these conversations at the margins of our material existence that matter and shape even the most mundane details of our daily lives.

But this is also a calling to acknowledge the <u>worlds</u> that we create through our <u>words</u>. Each poem and novel that an author <u>breathes</u> is a <u>birth</u> of a universe that continues to exist on its own, even after the author dies. This is the case both figuratively and literally as Derrida would concur. The only control authors have over their writings is that initial energy and intention with which they infuse every letter, period, question, and exclamation mark.

"But writers and their woes: they couldn't be parted. Not for anything."
– Naomi Wood

The power of intention is central to the creative process. *Himma* (intentive power) is a term that Ibn al-ʿArabi returns to often. He describes two ranks of sages according to the power of their *himma*. The lower can manifest their imaginal thoughts as physical entities simply by focusing their intentive power on a desired object. However, they must maintain their *nazar* (physical gaze) upon the object for it not to disappear. On the other hand, the higher-ranking saints need not maintain their <u>sight</u> on this <u>site</u>; it will remain in the physical world for as long as they will it to be.

Co-incidentally, Ibn al-ʿArabi retorts to this same process, of fixing the gaze upon an object, as the pretext to tell whether one is looking at a physical being or a *shabah* (ghost): the former can move freely out of <u>site</u>, even if we try to fix them under our <u>sight</u>, but the latter are imprisoned under the power of the gaze. Of course, the *himma* of the sage can affect not only the physical world, but also God, that is – at least – as He exists in the mind and heart of the human being.

This is in reference to the teaching of the prophet ﷺ where he states that

God says: "I am at my servant's opinion of Me. So, let them think well of me." The Sufi mystic emphasizes that this teaching is not a mere sentimental calling to have hope in divine mercy, but an active awareness of the fact that He is, for us, according to our *zann* (opinion) of Him. But let us not forget that God, the metacosmic *lahut*, is but a mirror of the macrocosmic and microcosmic divinity as well.

And so, whom we believe God and the universe to be, that is ultimately who we are. These three mirrors, as we mentioned, reflect one another verbatim, in levels of being, <u>verses</u> and <u>universes</u>. Here, Ibn al-ʿArabi references another central Sufi teaching that hearkens to the Oracle at Delphi: "Whoever knows themselves, knows their Lord." He also adds his own, stronger reformulation: "Whoever knows themselves has already known their Lord."

"All writers are vain, selfish, and lazy, and at the very bottom of their motives lies a mystery. Writing a book is a long, exhausting struggle, like a long bout of some painful illness. One would never undertake such a thing if one were not driven by some demon whom one can neither resist nor understand."
– George Orwell

In the Sufi cosmo-genesis, God spoke creation into being to reflect upon the beauty, perfection, and completion of His names and attributes. As we have reiterated throughout this book, this divine drama is an ancient predisposition in humanity. We also voice our innermost fears and hopes in art, specifically written words, that not only give *nafas* (breath) to the *nafis* (precious) meanings that reside in our *nafs* (soul), but also allow us to carry those stories to their natural conclusions, be they tragic or comedic.

I once gave a talk about the importance of storytelling in religious practice for a Muslim student organization at a university. After the lecture, one of the students approached me and asked: "Should I 'clean' my story before writing it, so that it does not have any profanities or darkness?" My response was very simple: "How would you know what profanities or darkness haunt your story, much less how to heal and exorcise them, if you have not written it yet?" We write to heal, not heal first before writing.

"To say that a writer's hold on reality is tenuous is an understatement – it's like saying the Titanic had a rough crossing. Writers build their own realities, move into them, and occasionally send letters home. The only difference between a writer and a crazy person is that a writer gets paid for it."
– David Gerrold

And here we find ourselves at an interesting juncture between the words of God that do not expire, external to us, and those that reside inside us. I feel as though the art of creative writing has willingly sacrificed itself, letters and all, for the author to deliver their burdens to its shores. We cast the net of our darkness into the ocean of ink so that we do not resort to channeling those inner demons on the words of God around us.

The protagonist, antagonist, plot, and setting of every story live inside of us. Here, I am reminded of the film *Identity*, directed by James Mangold, that follows six strangers who find themselves inside a deserted hotel during a severe storm. A series of murders take place. In the end, all these characters emerge as mere *ashbah* (sg. *shabah*. Ghosts) of a single individual who has a multiple personality disorder. Not to diminish from the magnitude of this mental illness, but all writers are – in some dimension – like Malcolm Rivers, with thousands of characters living their lives in a single person's imagination.

But I also would like us to entertain the hypothetical scenario where creative writing can be commonly used as a journey of healing for mental disorders, much like music was – and still is – utilized to cure the sick in Turkish hospitals. How much suffering could be alleviated, through the pen, to ink on paper; if not completely, then at least by exorcising our inner demons. Reminiscing on Ruth Stone who catches the galloping horse of her creative inspiration by the pen, pulling it back and singing it onto the canvas, let us imagine the inverse movement: to catch an inner snake that is wreaking havoc on our inner levels of <u>being</u>, <u>be-hold</u> it, and with our pen push it out of us onto a story's canvas.

"Good writers define reality; bad ones merely restate it. A good writer turns fact into truth; a bad writer will, more often than not, accomplish the opposite."
– Edward Albee

This visual of exorcising a snake was masterfully embodied in the TV show *Titans*, an adaptation of DC's younger generation of heroes. The character Conner Kent aka *Superboy*, played by Joshua Orpin, is infested by a dark-magical snake that is destroying his – otherwise – formidable composition. In comes another Titan Gar(field) Logan aka *Beast Boy*, played by Ryan Potter, whose superpower is transforming into various entities, including a tiger, snake, gorilla, bat, and in this case, a virus.

Logan willingly enters Kent's body as a microbe and coaxes the snake out of hiding, thereby healing his friend and eventually returning to the physical world with one fitting exclamation: "Now that, was a wild ride!" Indeed, it is. If only our pens could speak, and they do. It is an exhilarating myth to dive into our subconscious, to find memories there that we had <u>forgotten</u> and <u>forged</u> into rendered <u>foreigners</u> living inside. And it is so redeeming to deem them as fitting curves of ink in our stories, transporting them from one universe to another.

I have chosen to begin the second half of this book and these series of chapters on the different genres of art with writing because I believe it's metaphysically and pragmatically foundational. In the first instance, the incessant divine vibrations known as God's speech or words color our existence in hue, sound, and movement. For Ibn al-ʿArabi, the words of God are the spirits of all forms of human art. Like the ancient city of Iram, the metacosmic *lahut* creates through us. Rather, we are Him creating and His creative process itself. There is no difference, only deference.

> *"Raise your words, not your voice. It is rain that grows flowers, not thunder."*
> – Rumi

In the second instance, as Inayat Khan expresses, words seem to be the first creative *hayr* (fortress) for human beings to express their *hayra* (perplexity). Not only are novels and poems written in ink, but so are plays, films, and tv shows, just prior to coming to life through the *harakat* (accents/movements) of actors and directors. Even our architecture and music are first written down in their own languages; ones that hearken to ancient hieroglyphics and speak more than the eye can see.

The bodies of words and letters need the ornamentation of accents to come to life. Our writing humbly sends us towards other forms of art that are better fit to express the meanings that reside in our souls. Similarly, our *ruh* (spirit) also points the way to the bodily vessel as an essential, not trivial, carrier of meaning. Our corporeal suffering and redemption, in all its grandiosity and triviality, is the stuff of spirit. The metaphor animates meaning. Meanwhile, we cherish the show as we linger in-between.

The Turkish Sufi poet Yunus Emre says: "I tried to study the four scriptures [Psalms, Torah, Gospel, Qur'an]. But then love came, and it all became one syllable." Such are the artist-sages, in this case writer-sages, who expend their words/worlds to reach the summit of their craft. There, they find all their stories, poems, and novels waiting for them. All are silently speaking, moving in stillness, and living in death much like Ibn al-'Arabi's elapsed youth.

The Dye of God: On the Visual Arts

"This is the dye of God, and whose dye is more beautiful than God's?"
– Holy Qur᾿an (2:138)

I would like to begin with a known Sufi legend that beautifully shows the loving relationship between the two languages of letters and colors. There was once a town with a high wall. Everybody who tries to see what lies behind it leaves and never returns. Once, a wise guy in the town thought to tie a rope around his waist and ask the townspeople to hold the other end. As soon as he peeked beyond the wall, he tried to jump but the townspeople pulled him back. They asked him: "What did you see?" Unfortunately, the experience had rendered him a mute for the rest of his life.

I feel as though the distinction between languages and painting, photography, or drawing, as the mediums for written and visual arts is rather haphazard. As we saw in the previous chapter, there is nothing less artistic about the calligraphy of letters than the content of words they compose. Inversely, in this chapter, I would like us to appreciate the prospect of 'reading' the visual arts. To be able to interpret the metaphors of a painting by Picasso, architectural masterpiece by Zuha Hadid, or photograph by Ansel Adams is the holistic approach I am seeking in the following pages.

> *"We share a huge visual memory bank, mostly through painting and other images in history. I think when a modern photograph taps into those, sometimes very subliminally, it makes people respond."*
> – Chris Hondros

As mentioned in the preface, I am blessed to have been born into a family of entirely visual artists. My mother is a painter and interior decorator. My father, although an entomologist, is a nature-photographer. My brother is an architect and sister a pottery maker. My childhood, the same one that I described as orphaned of a motherland, is filled with memories of galleries in Baghdad's Saddam Center for the Arts and Amman's Royal Cultural Center where my father's and mother's work circulated, gathered, and garnered gazes.

My family's collective art production is as much a nostalgic safe space for me as all the memories associated with each of these works. Like my parents' galleries, seeing my brother's work at his university's student fair or my sister's pottery at her workplace, named *Silsal* (Pottery), in Amman are journeys that I involuntarily undertake every time I see, think, or even smell their works. This is but one of many ways in which visual art can be read like a journal that speaks in silence.

Al-Ghazali, who died only 40 years before Ibn al-ʿArabi, believed that our physical sights cannot be trusted because when we look at the sun, for instance, we believe it is no bigger than a coin, even though we know it is much larger. Ibn al-ʿArabi disagreed with his predecessor in *The Meccan Openings*, stating that our physical sights do not lie; they convey exactly what they see. Indeed, the sun is as big as a coin, as far as our pupils are concerned.

> *"Landscape painting is really just a box of air with little marks in it telling you how far back in that air things are."*
> – Lennart Anderson

However, the Sufi mystic contends that it is our ʿaql (rational faculty) that cannot be trusted, since it is the court that issues judgements on what the sensory faculties perceive. This is why, he insists, we must intellect with our *qulub* (sg. *qalb*, hearts) rather than minds. As mentioned previously, the ʿaql is <u>tethered</u> to ʿiqal (<u>leash</u>) and seeks to always categorize, <u>*hadd*</u> (define) and <u>*hadd*</u> (limit). On the other hand, the <u>*qalb*</u> (heart) is the companion of <u>*qalb*</u> (upending) and *taqallub* (fluctuations) that are more reflective and give the *haqq* (right) of the actual state of *haqiqa* (reality).

But I would like us to take Ibn al-ʿArabi's own statement further, what are the actual limits of our engagement with visual art? Can our eyes detect the sound of a building, smell of a painting, or vibration of a photograph? For the Sufi mystic, each sense has its limits, benefits, and shortcomings. However, we do know that they communicate with one another. Art, especially the visual kind, has the power to host all our faculties in a conversation.

It is a truly interdisciplinary spirit at the microcosmic level. Unlike our academies, where the sciences and humanities hardly communicate, a work of art instantly reminds a physical sense that there is also memory and imagination lurking somewhere in the darkness; all have much to benefit from one another.

Fortunately for our species, artists in our day and age are also the ones who ask the big questions on a macrocosmic level. For example, I do not think there has ever been a conversation between the sciences and humanities on the moral and ethical consequences of artificial intelligence. However, Steven Spielberg spearheaded that exact project in his masterpiece *AI: Artificial Intelligence* and asked the big questions, not only of science, but religion as well.

> *"You're creating interest in the foundation by creating those knowledge gaps, like in a novel, but not in a totally obvious way or it can get boring or trite."*
> – Clyde Aspevig

Since the conversation surrounding the social importance of art belongs to the final chapter, I would like to return here to the microcosmic interdisciplinary spirit of creativity. Focusing once again on the intimate mirroring between society and individual, Ibn al-ʿArabi compares the cosmic <u>faculties</u> (i.e., planets, stars, angels, sages) to our own inner <u>facilities</u>. Therefore, the five human senses are our inner planets and stars. The *ʿaql* (rational faculty) is our inner angel, whereas the *qalb* (heart) is the microcosmic sage.

How wondrous is it that one of our inner stars, the eyes, is the same <u>sense</u> we use to make <u>sense</u> of both the written and visual arts; yet, engaging with each of these forms gives birth to entirely different meanings in the heart. It is indeed as Ibn al-ʿArabi had said, the gaze simply conveys what it receives, and it is entirely up to whichever faculty that takes charge of this data to interpret and perceive it as it sees fit. However, the question remains, what is the role of our other senses in engaging with a painting, photograph, or building?

We had discussed in the previous chapter the importance of reading both the content and context of a book. To touch its grammar and body from cover to cover, all the while deciphering its memories, drafts and the journey that had guided it from a mere thought in the mind of an author to its final shape in our hands. The same can be said about any work in the visual arts. Are we perceptive enough to read the layers of dye effaced behind what was chosen by the painter as the final mark on the canvas?

"Architecture should speak of its time and place, but yearn for timelessness"
– Frank Gehry

The artist Phyllida Barlow perceives the importance of 'invisible' visual art that never sees the 'light' of day. Although it is produced by the artist, it is not shown at galleries. Such works play an important role in the journey of the painter: they are marks and traces in the trek towards the summit; abodes along the path where we do not actually take rest, only wrest whatever strength we have to keep going.

We should be asking how these dead ghosts of art haunt their descendants who do eventually see the light of day on canvas. Karl Marx expresses this idea beautifully: "The traditions of the dead linger like a nightmare on the minds of the living." Sometimes it is a nightmare, others an eloquent dream, a <u>knight's mare</u>. Or as the spirit of Luke Skywalker encourages his disciple Rey from beyond the vale: "The spirits of all the Jedi live in you now." Every work we produce not only proclaims our growth, but also whispers our shortcomings.

This is a return to the muhammadan reality and the gradual revelation of *al-insan al-kamil al-tamm* (perfect and complete human) in stages; a process that itself manifests in the artist-sage who expends every breath of their instrument, in this case brushstrokes and colors, to reach the summit of their craft where the singularity awaits. There, they perhaps will be able to peek beyond the wall and still voice it, unlike our misfortunate fool in the story at the beginning of this chapter.

"Art is a place for children to learn to trust their ideas, themselves and to explore what is possible."
– Maryann F. Kohl

Ibn al-ʿArabi uses the Qurʾanic story of Moses' birth to expound upon this motif of the haunting past and how it possesses the present. Pharaoh had been persecuting the first-born male children of the Israelites when their prophet was born and was ironically taken care of by the king of Egypt. The Sufi mystic explains that the incredible strength Moses had, which eventually led him to inadvertently kill another human being, was the cumulative power of all the murdered children of the Israelites, all of whom had been sacrificed so that this prophet of God could avenge them.

I would like us to venture into another conversation between Ibn al-ʿArabi and Moses before we re-turn to the significance on the side of art. The Sufi mystic focuses on the power that this prophet of God had, not only in adulthood, but also childhood. Indeed, he was more powerful in his *tabut* (lit. grave, basket) that carried him along the Nile to the pharaoh's palace. This is evident in the fact that the heart of the oppressor softened for Moses not when he was an adult, but rather an infant.

Where did this *quwwa* (strength) come from? Ibn al-ʿArabi tells us that it is an inherent power in infants who are able to bend the mind and will of adults to their own, making them feed, clean, and even play with their children as if they themselves had become infants once again. This insurmountable clout that newborn babies have, the Sufi mystic explains, is due to their innocence. However, he means this in a metaphysical, not sentimental, sense: infants are innocent because they have recently arrived from the unseen.

> *"The urge to draw must be quite deep within us, because children love to do it."*
> – David Hockney

Another relationship springs to heart here between the visual and written arts. This revolves around the Arabic homonym *hadith*, which means both speech – as in the teachings of the prophet ﷺ - and the adjective 'new' or 'recent'. In reference to the second definition, the prophet instructed his disciples to step out and expose their bare heads to rain because it is *hadith ʿahd bi-rabbih* (recently arriving from its Lord). The Qurʾan also admonishes people for preferring 'old' knowledge and understandings they have inherited from their teachers while neglecting the *dhikr muhdath* (recently arriving remembrance) from God.

Infants, like rain and remembrance, are recently arriving manifestations of innocence from their Lord. But more than that, they are also performative instances of divine speech. On this topic specifically, the Moroccan saint 'Abd al-'Aziz al-Dabbagh says that the reason why infants are unable to speak the language of 'grown ups' is because their memory of the unseen is still intact. If they were to divulge the secrets they knew, the entire physical world would be in disarray.

Not only that, but al-Dabbagh also explains that if adults were to see the dreams of infants, they would physically melt due to the spiritual power and ecstasy in these visions. The Moroccan mystic then concludes by stating that the language infants speak, which we call 'cute gibberish', is none other than the tongue of angels in the unseen world. He uses specific words such as *gaga* and *mumu*, the terms for God and water in the *malakut* respectively, as a proof of this wonder.

> *"Artists are just children who refuse to put down their crayons."*
> – Al Hirschfeld

This power of infancy, dormant in the image of Moses, comes full circle when Ibn al-'Arabi agrees with al-Dabbagh's understanding of the language of spirits. The former explains that the name Moses was given to the baby by the people of Pharaoh. When they found his *tabut* (grave/basket) at the riverbank of the Nile by a palm tree, they named him according to where they found him: *mu* (water) *sa* (tree). Incidentally, the name for Jesus in Arabic, *'Isa* differs from *Musa* only in the first syllable. This is not surprising since the son of Mary was also born under a palm tree. The first *'I,* refers to the oasis or desert where Mary secluded herself during his birth.

This deep dive into metaphysics returns us to Picasso's well-known advice about artists mentioned in previous chapters: "Every child is born an artist. The trick is how to remain an artist once we grow up." Unsurprisingly, Pablo himself drew with the innocence and *tilqaʾiyya* (spontaneity) of a child. Our mystic-sages, Ibn al-ʿArabi and al-Dabbagh, are in complete agreement with this artist-sage. But they also unveil for us the metaphysical foundations underlying this need to remain – artistically – a child.

If we think of the artist-sage as a 'spiritual child', then we must also speak of spiritual *ummiyya* (illiteracy). The prophet ﷺ is described in the Qurʾan as *al-nabiyyi al-ummiyyi* (the illiterate prophet), a description that is often misinterpreted as: he did not know how to read or write. While that is true, in a sense, there is a deeper spiritual type of illiteracy whereby he was not veiled by learned knowledge from the 'recently arriving' remembrance that is renewed at every moment, like everything else in the cosmos.

"As an architect, you design for the present, with an awareness of the past for a future which is essentially unknown"
– Norman Foster

And so, now we have a rich image of the artist-sage as a perfect and complete human, spiritually illiterate and one who speaks the language of spirits. They are filled with the strength of memories, and always open to the recently arriving rain of creative inspiration. This we add to the list we gleaned from the description of Mary in chapter one as a single-parent of her artwork, Jesus. All of this helps us return with a fuller vision to our earlier question about the visual arts and what they communicate beyond ink on paper.

Our introductory anecdote hinted towards the phenomenon that paintings, architecture, and photography – just to mention a few – communicate more than the commune of grammar. In *The Literature of al-Andalus*, Jerrilynn Dodds talks about the marvels of Andalusia, such as Alhambra, as 'readable' architecture. These unique structures tell the history of the region through carefully catered emblems that have imprinted themselves upon the body of the building, like the *kalimat* of existence.

> *"How often have I lain beneath rain on a strange roof, thinking of home."*
> – William C. Faulkner

When Muslims had overtaken southern Spain, they left all Christian marks on these buildings, such as crosses or paintings of Jesus and Mary. Then, when the Reconquista took place in the 15th century and Christians retook Andalusia, they followed the same method as their predecessors and left all Muslim signposts (e.g., crescents, Arabic calligraphy) intact. What emerges from this layering is suffering and redemption, defeat and triumph in physical artifacts that perform their meaning in solemn stillness.

This visible history in the visual story of Andalusia is no different than any human art read by the eyes of observers. As I mentioned, every effaced brush stroke haunts those colors granted life by the artist. Like Toni Morrison's *Beloved*, the past reminds the present of its tragedy and trajectory. Nostalgia cannot be monopolized by poetry and music; it also thrives in the soil of color and texture. But that is only one of many ways in which hues can speak more in silence than words.

Perhaps shapes, the basic elements that form the visual arts, are themselves primordial letters. It is no wonder that hermetic knowledge thrived at the time of ancient Egyptians when the written and visual arts were married. For one has to read not only what each hieroglyphic symbolizes, but also appreciate the emblem itself. This is precisely the tragic state of language in modernity: we no longer <u>read</u> <u>calligraphy</u>. This is also why the visual arts are so important: they remind us how to <u>reed</u> our inner <u>cartography</u>.

If, as Derrida states, the *secret attestation* of poetry is its 'performativity': the way in which meaning is communicated beyond the use of grammar and more so using rhyme and meter, then a painting, photograph, or building can perform at an even deeper level, in complete silence and stillness. One need not <u>speak</u> to be at the <u>peak</u>; it is art by simply being. In Sufism, this is regarded as a much higher state of *dhawq* (taste) than verbal expression.

> *"If I could say it in words there would be no reason to paint."*
> – Edward Hopper

This is in reference to the maxim: *lisan al-hal ablagh min lisan al-maqal* (the tongue of the spiritual state is more eloquent than that of verbal speech). One of my Sufi guides, Shaykh Hisham Kabbani, explains this in relation to dreams: "If somebody truly wants to communicate something to you, with the hope of moving you into action, they will do so in dreams. In the physical <u>world</u>, <u>words</u> often reach no further than the <u>ear</u>. But in the dream world, the <u>heart</u> <u>hears</u>." Just as al-Dabbagh describes children: they receive in visions what emblematically guides them in mind and spirit.

Not only does visual art perform in silence, but it also <u>evokes</u> and <u>provokes</u> emotions that words just cannot seem to imprison. The painter him or herself seems to be more vulnerably <u>present</u>; they are able to <u>present</u> the reader of their work with their bare-naked truth, in ways which they might be able to hide better using letters and grammar. But again, this explicit and vivid movement in visual art merely returns us as more capable *bricoleurs* who can better read both the body and soul of a novel or poem.

Here, I think of my father whose expertise in entomology shines subtly in his nature-photography. Whereas most photographers leave their houses not knowing what they will find at the park, hoping to be pleasantly surprised, he knows exactly what to expect. Based on the season and month of the year, he is certain of the insects and flowers that are thriving at the moment. Like Ibn al-ʿArabi's sages who know their macrocosmic destiny as a result of their microcosmic self-knowledge, a photographer-sage like my father is also in harmony with his craft.

> *"Sculpture is what you bump into when you back up to see a painting."*
> – Barnett Newman

Likewise, my mother can predict harmony or dissonance before it happens. More than that, she has painted people and scenes years before meeting them. For example, she drew a portrait of her best friend Kafi before ever seeing her in person. When she showed the painting to her colleagues at the Iraqi television where she worked, they were stunned that it looked so much like Kafi: they first met in art, then in person. This is an exquisite performance of being open to *l'avenir*, the recently arriving creative inspiration and origin of all things physical in the singularity of the spirit.

Years later, prior to traveling to Greece to spend time with Kafi, my mother also painted a seashore with rocks and seagulls. When she showed it to her friend, the one who was herself an embodied portrait from the past, she was astonished: the scene my mother had painted was nothing but a <u>séance</u> to an actual seashore in Greece. When my mother went to reunite with her friend, they both spent time on that beach. It was just as the Qur'an states: "Indeed, you will know its truth after some time."

My brother, the architect, who had to academically study his craft twice, due to the fact that his credits from Iraq's universities were not accepted in Jordan – another casualty of war – displays the luster of mastering his craft in different modes. Perhaps it is just the way that a muse of architecture works. Like his older peer Peter Cook, my brother Muhammad has been gifted lessons about life that were chiseled into his being piece by piece, each brick of advice with its mortar.

"The viewer brings something individual to the experience of any artwork."
– Olafur Eliasson

Like Cook, he understands that what takes the hand years to <u>master</u> is just enough time for the heart to <u>muster</u> at a moment's notice. He knows, like Arnold Schwarzenegger, that if you choose to have a backup plan B for your passion, then it is not really that meaningful to begin with. Sir Michael Caine said the same thing about acting: "If for you it is only a fulltime job, waste neither your time nor that of the craft. When I go home, I never leave my character on set."

Like acting, architecture requires movement, an essential trait of being that Ibn al-ʿArabi stated is married to perplexity. Unlike a visit to the museum, where you stand solemnly still at each work and only move when ready to migrate to another, with architecture you have to move within the art. With each step, you also transition with-out yourself. Between paintings or photographs and architecture we have the liminal sculpture, an altar that forces us to <u>turn</u> and <u>return</u> in admiration.

And then, we have visual art that behaves like architecture. The masterful Olafur Eliason makes art that can only be heard if the observer stands at the right place and time. These include a prism of light that only manifests through an artificial drizzle of water if you stand at a specific distance, or a kaleidoscope of panels that show the full spectrum of life's colors when the audience is present, not only in space, but also at the moment a chromatic light is turned on.

"You have to let the viewers come away with their own conclusions. If you dictate what they should think, you've lost it."
– Maya Lin

Eliason also shows the story of climate change through a congregation of icebergs that are placed in the middle of downtown Boston. As passersby invest emotionally in each of these exhibited guests, they slowly witness them melt. They feel the sadness, but also understand the emotion dormant in the larger picture: we have not collectively undertaken the journey to elevate ourselves through the three stages of Taal's delineation of faith, from solid to gas. In turn, we have projected this untold story violently upon the <u>words</u> of God in the <u>world</u>, namely nature.

There is much more wisdom to be deciphered here in Eliason's method. This artist's conviction that "reality is how we perceive it" can be found almost verbatim in Ibn al-ʿArabi's writings. We already have many of the pieces to understand the Sufi approach to this concept. As mentioned, he quotes an earlier Sufi mystic, al-Junayd, who when asked about gnosis said: "The color of water is that of its cup." Our awareness of the universe, and the art we produce therefrom, is itself like an unfolding painting in watercolor.

Ibn al-ʿArabi also told us that no form manifests to one person twice, nor once to two people. What all of this means is that knowledge and truth are necessarily individualized and subjective. And yet, the Sufi mystic is a vehement monotheist with a deep conviction in oneness and the divine singularity. Both of these approaches lead to a perception of truth that is contentiously subjectively-objective.

What I taste of truth and reality through my perceptions, dispositions, and experiences, although drastically different from even those people closest to me, is nonetheless the same singularity. This is precisely why we all need to seek the intimate self-knowledge that all beings have of the macrocosm and metacosmic *lahut*. The beautiful symbolism in the image of the heart as a cup with a specific color is that hues are additive and eventually accumulate to pure light.

> *"Failure with clay was more complete and more spectacular than with other forms of art. You are subject to the elements…Any one of the old four — earth, air, fire, water — can betray you and melt, or burst, or shatter — months of work into dust and ashes and spitting steam."*
> — A.S. Byatt, *The Children's Book*

Ibn al-ʿArabi calls this individualized and unique gnosis that each being has of truth and reality the *wajh khass* (private countenance), in contrast to the *wajh ʿamm* (universal countenance) that describes the communal discourse about being and our place in existence. No one has access to the intimate conversations we each have with our inner and external *lahut*, but we can still learn it from one another, through the colorful prism of our own cups.

My sister Abeir has shown her trek up the summit through the discipline that clay has taught her through the years. A piece of pottery cannot be forced into submission; it demands a gentle guidance. Each successful piece of art at her workplace reminds of the way God created the first human, Adam in the Qur'an: "I molded Him with my own hands" and "He created the human being from a resonant clay like pottery." The holy spirit could not coerce the Word of Jesus into Mary. Likewise, the tranquility of our imagination follows an orbit like the seasons of our lives.

"I rarely end up in the place I think I'm going because the clay has its own ideas. I like the feeling of being led by the materials"
— Jami Porter Lara

My sister's work remains here and there. I see it and remember the memories that speak through its texture and cracks in its walls. These, I think to myself, must be the same fissures that haunt the effaced image of my grandparents' house in Baghdad. It is a wonder that I held these same objects over twenty years ago. I am convinced that an imprint of my younger self is still there someplace on this mug or that pot. This is the power of art.

I reenacted this miracle once while taking my morning walk around the parking lot of my apartment. As I completed each lap in the snow, my footsteps traced a history. My previous selves remain, and I am left wondering, like readers of my photograph, whether these steps sing of different people or one person just a moment prior. Perhaps, as Ibn al-'Arabi would say, you are never yourself a moment ago. What is important is that photography can transform a walk in the blistering cold into art.

My sister learned to guide the contours of her creative life from an old teacher, clay. She adapted to making jewelry, learning to listen to precious stones tell stories of how they came to be and where they would like to go next, just as a primordial piece of clay whispers in the ear of the artist what it wishes to become. You see, you can read art not only to learn about its life, but also – and more importantly – yours as well.

I transition to another artist in my life before concluding this chapter with some self-reflection. My wife, Fatima Nazan, is the perfect example of an artist who has maintained her childhood and *ummiyya* (spiritual illiteracy). When our guide, Shaykh Hisham Kabbani, introduced us he told me: "She is a person of *dhawq* [taste]." That has shown in so many ways, perhaps most clearly in her ability to translate motherhood into crafts made from wool-felt that not only reflect innocence but speak the very ocean of spirituality across which infants sail to the shore of *nasut.*

"From what we get, we can make a living; what we give, however, makes a life."
– Arthur Ashe

She first began by making a baby mobile for our daughter Zahra that then developed into exquisite exhibits that orbit above a sleeping child, reminding them of 'home'. A few years later, she made a group of dolls as gifts for the kids during Eid, our communal Muslim celebration after the completion of the month of fasting, Ramadan. This also developed into countless dolls from wool-felt that resemble Sufi sages performing their child-like innocence after reaching the summit.

What is most notable about my wife's journey with her craft(s) is that it always began from a place of selflessness. She neither started making baby mobiles and dolls to make money nor become famous. She made them as gifts and was – in turn – gifted. She was granted not only the energy or motivation to keep producing, but more importantly the innocence and child-like aura of strength that still embraces her work.

My wife has since stopped making dolls, but the innocence remains in other projects that she has undertaken since then. Whether it is a storybook with miniature paintings or a children's book adaptation of the *mawlid* (celebration of the prophetic birth), the sense of motherhood makes its presence known on every page, image, and letter. Hers is a meaning that continues to unfold in different *suwar* (forms). All one has to do is be silent and listen for the moment to arrive, then to thrive in action.

> *"All art is a gift. It is first of all a gift that the maker can do it."*
> – Vincent Van Gogh

For an artist, the importance of accepting the gift when it arrives cannot be overstated. Another teacher of mine, Habib ʿUmar tells a story about the sage Ibrahim b. al-Adham, who was known for his *zuhd* (asceticism). He struggled with his ego and sought to wean it away from every desire. For 20 years, he chiseled away at his love for a particular dessert. One day, while walking in the marketplace, a man came to him with a tray full of that same delicacy. Ibrahim cried to the dismay of the man. "Why are you crying?" he asked, "because I worked so hard to rid myself of this desire, and you come now to destroy all that I have accomplished."

"Know that I am a messenger from God", the man said, "and He sends me to you with a message: 'whoever is gifted and does not accept, there will come a time that they will ask, but will not be given.'" Like Elizabeth

Gilbert, who had to involuntarily forsake her story about the Amazon, sages of all colors must accept the fact that the ocean never stops ebbing and flowing. We either catch the wave or miss it and have to wait for the next cycle.

I come alongside you to the conclusion of this chapter with a better understanding of the visual arts in my past and present. I find myself in-between the crafts of writing, photography, music, and the art of writing about all of them. Three of these genres we have discussed, while music will be our focus in the next chapter. As I reflect on the two art forms we have discussed so far, written and visual, I find myself drawn into the notion of movement, whether temporally or spatially, through and within a work.

If a miracle, as al-Ghazali has defined, is that which breaks the habitual, then how wondrous is a painting in front of which we stand frozen like a block of ice, yet inwardly are melting into our past memories like a newly arriving remembrance. Those sculptures around which we orbit like a loving moon or buildings between which walls we travel, they perform the impossible. They open a channel for an ascension, from the physical *nasut* towards the *lahut*.

The visual arts may or may not convey any more meanings than their written siblings, but what they definitely do teach us is how to read the body of language, that primordial force that communicates at the level of infants, they who embody in their strength and innocence the fresh remembrance of creativity rushing towards us like ships of stone across a sea of sand, or a galloping horse down the hills in rural Virginia.

The *Sawt Sarmad*: On the Auditory Arts

"Where words fail, music speaks."
– Hans Christian Andersen

After the *munshid* (religious singer) chanted some odes in a large gathering at the house of Habib 'Umar b. Hafidh in Tarim, Yemen, the sage says: "The reason human beings love beautiful voices and sounds is because it reminds them of the day that God spoke to them. On that day of *alastu bi-rabbikum* [am I not your Lord], we all heard the call. Thus, beautiful voices remind us of the divine address – [the *sawt sarmad*, eternal sound]. This is why we are moved emotionally."

The first experience I had being moved to tears by sound was in Jordan. I must have been 10 years old when my father took me to the local *masjid* (mosque) for the Friday sermon. The *mu'adhdhin* (caller to prayer) melodiously recited the *adhan* (call to prayer) in such a way that I felt my heart ripped to pieces. I knew nothing about Arabic music at the time, but recognized that the melody in which the artist had chanted was particularly somber.

Years later, in 2004 while memorizing the Qur'an, I was exposed to a deeply rich heritage on my mother's – Egyptian – side. I began learning the ocean of Arabic music known as *maqam* modal theory. This term is enough to guide us throughout this chapter. The word *maqam* has at least three deeply spiritual meanings: a spiritual station that we discussed previously, a shrine of a saint, and a modality of Arabic music.

> *"We have barely scratched the ocean of maqam music."*
> – Simon Shaheen

When I eventually picked up the oud in 2017, after years of learning Western music on the piano and guitar, I found my <u>entirety</u> <u>embodied</u> in this instrument. The oud is the perfect example of a *barzakh* (liminal interstice) between east and west. This ancestor of the guitar migrated, like me, from Baghdad to Spain sometime in the 11th century, at the hands of a celebrated Iraqi musician named Ziryab.

The oud, also like me, can speak two tongues: Arabic and Western music. Many of my American friends are surprised when I tell them that the guitar imprisons me: <u>frets</u> <u>feel</u> like those border officers in Middle Eastern countries who refuse to let you cross from one country to another. "But how do you remember where to put your fingers on the strings without frets?" My response to this question is always: "The same way I've treaded my entire life, by submitting."

Maqam music is a safe space; a shrine where I can entomb myself in seclusion for a while. I willingly give the oud my memories, and it gifts me emotions in return. But as I hold my instrument and listen to its vibrations, I also find myself gently forced into silence. Perhaps the only time I can remain quiet for hours is when the oud is speaking. Musical instruments, more so than the tools of any other craft, are living sages that involuntarily draw reverence out of us.

Ibn al-ʿArabi talks about divine union in terms of *hadith*, a term we discussed in the previous chapter that means both 'speech' and 'new'. He states that when one enters the presence of *lahut* they are either a *muhaddith* (speaker) or *muhaddath* (spoken to), but not both. If you want to speak, He will listen. And if you want Him to respond, you will have to be silent. When a musician holds their instrument, they agree to empty – in stillness – all the burdens that fill their <u>cup</u>. Then, they must allow their wooden sage to pour the <u>cure</u> in vibrations.

> *"Music is the silence between the notes."*
> – Claude Debussy

One of my oud teachers, the incredible Palestinian virtuoso Ahmad al-Khatib once told me that one of his teachers advised him to close his eyes while playing the oud. He should imagine that he is both blind and mute while music is the only medium he knows how to communicate with the universe. Speak your <u>heart</u> out with your hands and listen with your <u>ear</u>, to that same <u>art</u> you are voicing. Music teaches us that, at the summit, it is more about <u>reducing</u> you to nothingness than <u>producing</u> a work.

Let us return to the wonder of a musical instrument as a saint or sage. When I think of the oud or Turkish reed-flute, the nay, I cannot help but imagine a being that has completed their *suluk* (self-discipline). Both these instruments are separated from their homes, the tree bark and reedbed respectively. The wood is <u>burned</u> and <u>broken</u> into discipline. Thenceforth, that inner cup known as the body is emptied and made <u>hollow</u>. Lastly, <u>holes</u> are made in the body that allow <u>holy</u> breath and sound to dance both within and without the instrument.

"Music is a spiritual thing; you don't play with music. If you play with music, you will die young. You see, because when the higher forces give you the gift of music, it must be well used for the gift of humanity."
– Fela Kuti

We have spoken about our heart as a cup that colors and shapes the water of truth, but musical instruments show us the way to a higher reality still. The only reason these wooden sages can produce music is because they're more than simply containers, rather channels. They allow breath to flow through without imprisoning any of it, like those border officers. And how selfless is the oud or nay? When the hands of a musician voice <u>memories</u> through them, in a sonorous <u>remembrance</u>, the audience does not thank the instrument, but the artist.

Even though it is the instrument that has done the hard work, of channeling breath and heat, it does not complain. It neither seeks acknowledgment nor <u>ovation</u>. The only thing it demands is sincerity and honesty in your <u>vocation</u>. Playing a musical instrument is not an empty <u>vacation</u>. It is a <u>vicarious</u> attempt to know how to be and do nothing. It is to internalize what it means to be like a dead body in the hands of a divine musician. You hold back nothing of the sacred breath, rather let it all go. Most importantly, you are content with the gift of effacement.

A musician, unlike Jack Lemon, does not need a film director to tell them to 'do less!'. The instrument will never open its heart to the artist, even after many years of companionship, if they enter the temple of music with a speck of dishonesty. Do not just empty your cup but <u>destroy</u> it if you want to tell your <u>story</u>. "This journey will break you", the instrument whispers, but is there a more beautiful way to be <u>sundered</u> than through a <u>sonorous</u> lullaby?

This lesson of selflessness that a musical instrument seeks to transmit to the artist can be learned in the life of the sage-scholar Muhammad b. Idris al-Shafi'i, a Muslim polymath and founder of one of the four schools of law in Islam. He is narrated to have asked God that his teachings spread across east and west but not in his name, rather through others. This is the same selflessness embedded in the oud and nay. They adamantly echo that primordial divine speech, the *sawt sarmad*, while at the same time never claiming to be the source – much less the channel – of these vibrations.

> *"You can play a shoestring if you're sincere."*
> – John Coltrane

We had discussed the four stages of mastering a craft in a previous chapter, from 'unconsciously incompetent' to 'unconsciously competent', or as Ibn al-'Arabi described it earlier, from the darknesses of ignorance to the darkness of *hayra* (perplexity). This latter stygian paradox manifests musically in the tension between the imperative of doing nothing to receive everything. The journey in this artform is from <u>assuming control</u> to a <u>subsuming whole</u>.

A great example of this can be found in a story related by another oud virtuoso, the Jordanian musician Tariq al-Jundi. In the early years of his journey with the oud, like many other beginners, he sought to become a master of technique. Thus, he learned a difficult piece known as a *capris* by the Turkish oudist Şerif Muhittin Targan. He proudly played the composition in front of an old oud master during an audition for admission at the musical academy in Jordan.

Al-Jundi played the piece perfectly while his teacher listened attentively. Afterwards, the sage said something that al-Jundi described as obliterating: "Tariq, it is good to hear some musicians, while others it is better to only see them. Which of the two do you want to be? When you are 50 or 60 years old and have arthritis, do you think you will still be able to play with this same flexibility?" The teacher then picked up the oud and played an improvisation with few notes. Al-Jundi was moved to silence, much more quickly than his own display of finesse playing the *capris*.

> *"A legend is an old man with a cane known for what he used to do. I'm still doing it."*
> – Miles Davis

Ahmad al-Khatib also speaks about this <u>lesson</u> in <u>lessening</u> when he mentions a story that his father, a Palestinian poet, had taught him about *balagha* (eloquence). The musician told me this story after I asked him: "Your plucking of the string is so meticulous and clear that I cannot imagine you striking any other note than the one you intended, how did you learn to play like this?" He said that his father had once asked him: "Ahmad, do you know what eloquence is? It is the ability to convey a meaning in as few precise words as possible such that there can be no mistake in the mind of the listener regarding your intention."

The paradox here is not only that a musician has to be nothing to channel everything, but they also have to cease gently, to disappear without being noticed. The annihilation of ego should not haunt the performance. It must not speak from beyond the vale as is the case with the visual and written arts. If a poem represents the *shari'a* (law) of self-knowledge, a painting its *tariqa* (path), then a piece of music is the *fana'* (annihilation) of self that eventually delivers one to the shore of *haqiqa* (reality).

"After silence, that which comes nearest to expressing the inexpressible is music."
– Aldous Huxley

Returning to the Qur'an, a divine address to the prophet David and his community alludes to the precious gnosis conveyed through music: "Work, oh people of David in gratitude. Indeed, very few of my servants are grateful" (34:13). It is narrated that when the prophet ﷺ heard his disciples recite the Qur'an in a beautiful voice, he would complement them by saying: "You have been gifted a reed-flute like that given to the people of David."

The knowledge given to the prophet David is instrumental in understanding the primacy of music and knowledge of sound in Sufism. Ibn al-'Arabi explains that the first scripture, which was given to David (e.g., Psalms) was nothing but music. It is the primordial revelation. Prior to the Word, there was the <u>humming</u> of the divine <u>hymn</u>. The Sufi mystic extrapolates from this sacred history that music is the original form of speech. When a continuous sound is disconnected, fluctuated in pitch, and pronounced from different *maqamat* (stations) in our vocal system, it is reborn as human speech.

It is for this reason that the 11th century Arab philosopher al-Farabi says in his masterpiece *The Great Book of Music* that the best instrument is the human voice. He describes spectacular Muslim musicians who lived in present-day Mecca and Medina, at a time when music was still thought of as a sacred art. One of these sages wore bells that covered his entire body. When he wanted to produce a particular melody, he knew exactly which body part to shake in order to produce the desired sound.

> *"I play the notes as they are written, but it is God who makes the music."*
> – Johann Sebastian Bach

Likewise, Naser Dumairieh shows in *The Intellectual Life in the Hijaz Before Wahhabism* that until the 18th century there were prominent scholars and sages living in this region who not only taught musical theory but were themselves musicians. If modernity had rendered religion a private space, that other side of secularism as Talal Asad describes, then it has also deprived faith of the necessary means to <u>express</u> a spiritual <u>experience</u>. This much can be easily gleaned from the Wahhabi incursion on Islam.

Returning to the Qur'an, the image of the musician who learns how to become nothing from their instrument is succinctly described in the aforementioned verse of scripture where the prophet David and his community are called to tread the path of *shukr* (gratitude). As we discussed earlier, in Sufism, *shukr* is juxtaposed against *zuhd* (asceticism), the path of rigorous self-renunciation. Despite the prevalence of the latter among many practitioners, al-Dabbagh states that the path of saints is the former.

We have already seen the ruse of *zuhd* in the story of Ibn al-Adham previously, but al-Dabbagh explains it better. As a seeker takes on the frugal lifestyle of an ascetic, they might receive spiritual gifts and wrongly assume that it was their struggle and hard work that yielded this fruit. However, in reality, there is nothing a seeker can do to merit receiving the unseen. As we have seen throughout this book, our struggles at the prayer mat and studio alike cannot force the hand of our hidden treasure.

"I inhaled the fragrance of cedar as fresh as the first day that I acquired the guitar. And a voice seemed to say to me, 'you are an old man and you have not said thank you; you have not brought your gratitude back to the soil from which this fragrance arose.' And so, I come here tonight to thank the soil and the soul of this people that has given me so much."
– Leonard Cohen

We work in gratitude to acknowledge that our hidden treasure has made itself known in the past and to proclaim our conviction that it will speak again. But al-Dabbagh extends the horizon of *shukr* even further. When he tells his student that it is a lowly aspiration for a disciple to pray only for reward, the latter asks if seeking *qurba* (nearness) instead is the correct intention. The teacher says it is better, but still not the ideal goal because there remains the hidden pride and assumption that the power to pray is inherent in us, while in reality, as the Qur'an says: "He created you and all that you do" (37:96), and "He is the One who prays upon you" (33:43).

Another Moroccan sage, Mawlay ʿAbdul Salam b. Mashish, teaches his student the famed saint Abu Hasan al-Shadhili the same lesson about being nothing on the path of *shukr*. He asks: "My son, through what do you enter upon God?", "Through my *faqr* [poverty] master" al-Shadhili responds. "My son, then you have entered upon Him with the greatest idol. Instead, enter to His presence through Him." *Zuhd* is to assume that we can do something to achieve anything, while *shukr* is the realization that we are nothing, yet blessed to receive everything.

This is the quintessential lesson that music teaches, to be nothing in the presence of the sage known as the instrument, and to do so humbly. As Fela Kuti poignantly expressed in the quote above, if you <u>play around</u> with music, as opposed to letting it <u>play</u> you into a <u>prayer</u>, you will not be able to continue this journey. It is a sacred craft, perhaps the most sacred of all. As we saw with the visual arts, which allow us to appreciate reading the calligraphy of language as well as grammar, the auditory arts show us the importance of being nothing, not only in music, but all arts as well.

"If, while at the piano, you attempt to form little melodies, that is very well; but if they come into your mind of themselves, when you are not practicing, you may be still more pleased; for the internal organ of music is then roused in you. The fingers must do what the head desires; not the contrary."
– Robert Schumann

Transitioning slightly to the importance of melody, the prophet's ﷺ complement to his disciples about their beautiful voices hearkens to another of his teachings, where he proclaims that "they are not from us, those who do not melodiously recite the Qur'an." Melody is not mere ornament or embellishment, but a key that unlocks meaning. The very grammar of the Islamic scripture is hidden behind the door of a *maqam*.

Unlike Western music, which relies heavily on harmony, its Arabic sibling focuses instead on melody and utilizes *zakhrafa* (ornamentation) techniques to add depth. The reason for this, as explained by Simon Shaheen, is because Arabic music has an abundance of available sounds. Not only tones and half-tones, but also microtones that reside in-between, like a *barzakh* where all emotion lives. It is this microtonality in Arabic music that gives it the exotic sound heard by the Western ear.

I later discovered that the *maqam* I had heard as a ten-year-old in Jordan is called *hijaz*, one of seven main *maqamat* that mirror many seven-fold frameworks in Sufism: God has seven main attributes, seven circumambulations around the Ka'ba during pilgrimage, and seven *lata'if* (subtleties or chakras) in the human being. In the case of the seven *maqamat* of Arabic music, these are the primary springs of emotion through which both <u>player</u> and listener may engage in <u>prayer</u>.

> *"Music touches us emotionally, where words cannot."*
> – Johnny Depp

Arabic music has two *maqamat* that evoke sadness, *hijaz* and *saba*. I should mention beforehand that there is a huge debate among Arab musicians as to whether any specific *maqam* can be associated with an emotion, since it is a rather culturally-subjective association and the melody that makes a people joyous will make others somber. Nevertheless, I speak to you from my own experience and feelings that have been ignited into life by each of these *maqamat*.

Saba in Sufism is known as the 'youthful wind of the east', a breeze from the side of the beloved that increases the lover's pain of separation and reminds them of their longing. This anguish of love is felt in every tone and microtone that the *maqam* breathes in voice and string. As for *hijaz*, it is a climactic itinerary of melodies that performs the height of a tragedy or drama. Qur'an reciters usually use this *maqam* at the summit of a story, where everything prior has led and all moments going forward descend towards a crescendo.

Maqam bayyati is the musical home where all adventures begin and end. Hence, reciters usually start and conclude their performances with this modality. It is a *maqam* that performs nostalgia in its very name: *bayyati* which is a derivative of *bayt* (home). In between, one also finds *maqam rast*, a majestic tonal family that sings of dominion and power. Meanwhile, ʿ*ajam* (foreign) is the joyous major scale from Western music that has found itself eastward. Lastly, *Maqam nihawand* and *sika* are celebratory stations that mingle nostalgia with joy.

> *"There's a melody in everything. And once you find the melody, then you connect immediately with the heart."*
> – Carlos Santana

Moreover, these *maqamat* are all related; the emotion of one delivers the listener to the other. This concept of *naqla* (modulation) does wonders in storytelling. The celebrated Qurʾan reciter Mustafa Ismail, known as *amir al-naghamat* (the prince of melodies), because he never recited a verse twice in the same scale – following Ibn al-ʿArabi's maxim: 'there is no repetition in creation' –, masterfully allowed *maqamat* to use his voice to unlock the meanings of God's speech.

In one such instance, he uses *maqam saba* while reciting verses that recount prophet Noah's supplication to God: "Oh my Lord, I am defeated, so be victorious." He begins from the lower octave, known as *qarar* (base) and then, when the divine response comes: "We opened the doors of heavens with avalanching water", he begins from the higher octave, *jawab* (response) and descends back to *qarar*, musically symbolizing the ascension from *nasut* to *lahut* and the returning descent.

He repeats the verse again, this time modulating from *saba* to *'ajam* at the precise moment when God responds. In this way, the heart wrenching supplication of Noah, ushered in brokenness, is met with the joy of the divine answer and victory. If Mustafa Ismail is the sage of melody in Qur'an recitation, his counterpart is Riyad al-Sunbati, the saint of oud. The latter has an exquisite series of recorded *taqasim* (sg. *taqsim*, improvisation) in various *maqamat*. His particular performance of *hijaz* is poignant. After exploring the full range of the *maqam* in a dazzling climax, he returns the listener for a few brief moments back home, to *bayyati*.

"Music evokes so many feelings in us, memories, nostalgia, things that are connected to our past."
– Olga Kurylenko

In those blinks of nostalgia, all the troubles and tensions unfolded by *hijaz* seem to dissipate. Interestingly, Sunbati's other *taqsim* in *bayyati* where he modulates briefly to *hijaz* does not have the same effect, on me at least. I wondered about the reason, and then found my inner *lahut* responding: "You are a migrant, so ask yourself: is longing for home stronger into diaspora or if one were always there, just taking a few excursions prior to a return?" Indeed, a single moment of redemption is enough to end suffering's lifelong oppression.

In *Immortal Beloved*, a biographical film about Beethoven, the composer – played by Gary Oldman – questions an enthusiast who is obsessed with his music about this artform as they both listen to one of his compositions: "Music is a dreadful thing, what does it do?", his interlocutor responds: "It exalts the soul". The musician interjects:

Nonsense! when you hear a marching band, are you

exalted? No, you march. When you hear a waltz, you dance. It is the power of music to carry one into the mental state of the composer. It is like hypnotism. So, what is going on in my mental state when I wrote this? A man is trying to reach his lover in a storm. His carriage is stuck in the mud. His lover will only wait so long. This is the sound of his agitation.

Could this anguish have been conveyed through words? If so, how many books does it take to describe the pain of separation? Music is, as Ibn al-ʿArabi defined it, the origin of speech. The Sufi mystic introduced almost every chapter of his two books, *The Meccan Openings* and *Bezels of Wisdom* with few verses of poetry that succinctly state what might have taken hundreds of pages of prose to explain.

> *"To play a wrong note is insignificant; to play without passion is inexcusable."*
> – Ludwig van Beethoven

In turn, one single musical note played with sincerity is enough to make volumes of poetry surrender at the altar of emotions. But as I listen to Beethoven's own *Moonlight Sonata* or the *taqasim* of al-Sunbati, Farid al-Atrash, Simon Shaheen, or Ahmad al-Khatib I also recognize that there are many more emotions that words and colors simply cannot convey. What are those feelings exactly? Well, if I could describe them in words, then I would have betrayed my own conviction that, as Hans Andersen stated, 'where words fail, music speaks'.

Indeed, it is best to be a *muhaddath* (addressee) when in the presence of this craft. It is not enough to be silent outwardly, but also inwardly, listening attentively with all our levels of being. This is the Qurʾanic prerogative of *istimaʿ* (attentive listening), as opposed to just *samaʿ*, which means both audition and hearing. Whereas hearing might be involuntary, *istima'* is intentional. In one particular verse, there emerges the added level of internal listening, *insat*: "And if the Qur'an is recited, then *istami'u* [listen attentively] to it and *ansitu* [be silent internally]" (7:204).

This is <u>nothing</u> but another way to be <u>nothing</u>. Between the <u>instrument</u>'s <u>instruction</u> to cease one's will, listening and playing with sincerity outwardly, and also inwardly with complete stillness, it is clear that music, as the highest echelon of the auditory arts, could very well be considered the *lahut* and hidden treasure among all artforms, simply because it demands annihilation in exchange for *baqa'* (subsistence).

> *"The memory of things gone is important to a jazz musician."*
> – Louis Armstrong

One of the most powerful experiences I had listening to music, and as a result becoming nothing, happened some years ago during my doctoral studies at the University of Michigan. I was working as a graduate assistant for a class on Arab cultures. I developed a habit of letting students listen to a sample of Arabic music at the beginning of every session. One day, for no apparent reason, I chose an instrumental oud composition by the Iraqi oudist Naseer Shamma.

This particular piece was called *'Amiriyya*, commemorating the bombing of a shelter in a neighborhood of Baghdad with that namesake during the First Gulf War. This shelter, simply given the number 25, was one among many that housed 400 women, children, and the elderly. American warplanes claimed that it was a storehouse for weapons. However, the only proof of what whispered inside were shadows that still burn on the walls, reminding of incinerations and final thoughts.

I began listening to the piece with my students. Slowly, my body started to shut down. The entire day, even after returning home, I could neither speak, cry, nor laugh. The only part of me still awake was a voice asking an obsessive series of questions: why did I survive as a six-year-old child when so many others my age had perished? What is the wisdom of America painfully pushing me into its arms, away from my place of birth? Lastly, and most importantly, I addressed the ghosts of the deceased: what can I do for you?

"Music brings a warm glow to my vision, thawing mind and muscle from their endless wintering."
– Haruki Murakami

Perhaps like Peter Cook's architectural hand, it took my heart and mind an entire day to comprehend the power of music. I finally received an answer from the spirits of shelter 25: "What can you possibly do for us? We are in a much better place than you. Do for yourself and keep our memory alive. Do not let us be forgotten." This was the first time I understood what Fela Kuti meant: "Do not play around with music."

I went through this same experience a second time, almost a year later during a visit to Senegal. We journeyed to the Island of Gorée, and the infamous 'door of no return'. We saw each prison cell that housed enslaved and tortured Africans before they were forced onto ships. Some refused and jumped into the ocean. The water still <u>remembers</u>; it recorded their memories, the oppression they faced, and recounted it back to us in clear anger.

I found myself again, founded. I asked the spirits the same questions and they gave me identical responses. This time, however, they asked me to sing for them an ode by the Moroccan sage Muhammad b. al-Habib. It is a long poem describing annihilation in the divine presence, rendered in *maqam bayyati.* It was the perfect performance of returning truly home, back to nothingness. I thought I was gifting this ode to the dead, only to realize as I wept, that it was the truly living who had granted me a grafted cure.

> *"I like beautiful melodies telling me terrible things."*
> – Tom Waits

Having spoken of the power of music when it speaks alone, I would like to transition now to how melody enlivens the written arts. We have touched upon this briefly in relation to the Qur'an, but more needs to be said about the dance between this ancestral artform and its descendant, speech. Music not only unlocks meanings inherent in grammar and content, but also shows us how to read body and context, a challenge that we highlighted in the previous two chapters.

I was once listening to a Sufi ode containing these heart wrenching sentiments: "My Lord, I am not fit for paradise, nor am I strong enough to withstand the fire." Despite the somber emotion evoked by the words, the *maqam* used was ʿ*ajam,* the quintessential modality of joy in Arabic music. I wondered about the wisdom in mixing happiness and sadness. It was only when I understood the history of the author did the story of his ode's music make sense.

The writer of these words was not a celebrated sage, but a hedonistic poet by the name of Abu Nuwwas who was born in Persia and later moved to Baghdad. He apparently never prayed and was a drunkard. And yet, in a few moments of brokenness, he had composed those words. They were divinely accepted and commemorated by sages a thousand years later. The happy ʿ*ajam* <u>remembers</u> the poet's lifestyle, while the words <u>remind</u> of his inner anguish.

I also realize that inner pain is much more vivid when hidden behind a tearful smile's mask, rather than a frown. These words of the Egyptian diva Umm Kulthum's song *Lissa Faker* (Do you still think…) are also sung in ʿ*ajam*: "Do you still think my heart will grant you safety, or do you still think one word can render things the way they were, or maybe one gaze can connect longing with mercy? Do you still think? No, this has passed". How much more meaning can be conveyed when melody <u>smiles</u> for <u>miles</u> in the blood of agony?

> *"Go easy on me, baby*
> *I was still a child*
> *Didn't get the chance to*
> *Feel the world around me*
> *I had no time to choose*
> *What I chose to do*
> *So go easy on me."*
> – Adele, *Easy on Me*

One musician whom I believe annihilates both audience and words through her voice is Adele. When I listen to her earlier songs, *Someone Like You* and *Hello*, I cannot help but find the universality of music tethering her emotionally to another diva from the East, Fairuz. The latter's song

Keifak Inta (How are you?) tells the same story. However, when I listened attentively to Adele's newest work, *Easy on Me*, I found myself weeping as I did at the 'door of no return' and in the company of residents from shelter 25.

I was transported, from Adele's own struggles and rites of motherhood that inspired these words, to myself standing before God for reckoning and singing my <u>pain</u> away with the <u>paint</u> of her lyrics. Then, there <u>turned</u> and <u>returned</u> the same divine response: "How would I not show mercy to a prayer sung so beautifully?" Motherhood and God's mercy converge in a teaching of the prophet ﷺ where he asks his disciples: "Do you think a mother would give her infant to ruin? Know that God is more merciful with His creation than a mother is with her child."

"When I hear music, I fear no danger. I am invulnerable. I see no foe. I am related to the earliest times, and to the latest."
– Henry David Thoreau

Perhaps that is all that music seeks from and for us: to return to infancy. This seems to be a universal advice by all artists, from Picasso to Adele. Ibn al-ʿArabi states that saints never ask God for mercy save by invoking His name *al-Rahman* (The Most-Merciful), because they do not simply want mercy to descend, but more importantly to become springs of mercy for all creation. This is the strength inherent in infants that turns everyone around them into children as well.

Like infants, a musical instrument has that power. It is sinless and speaks the language of spirits. Music is the summit for which we have been hoping throughout this book; the gaseous state of faith that turns one into "air …

thin air", to use Shakespeare's words. It is the *haqiqa* at the peak. Those who have struggled their way to the summit can now mingle in a universal language that is the origin of speech, yet beyond it altogether. And how wondrous is it that what lies at the top is nothing but a siren song!

The Reel of Reality: On the Moving Arts

"Cinema is a medium that can translate ideas."
– David Lynch

Ibn al-ʿArabi explains that our physical world perishes at every moment and is recreated again. This incessant annihilation and resurgence happen so organically that one perceives the illusion of continuity. In other words, our <u>reality</u> is a <u>reelity</u>. Every frame in our life is a snapshot of existence. This concordance between film, its predecessor theater, and the fabric of being is perhaps why the moving arts was – and still is – considered the most sacred of artforms, one that brings together the written, visual, and auditory crafts.

But nowadays, film and theater have a third sibling that shares the responsibility of serious storytelling: video games. With the advancement in technology, this genre of virtual narratives is no longer limited to two dimensional platformers like Super Mario or Pac-Man, but stories that actually rival television and cinema in their ability to coax an emotional engagement from viewers with characters and plot. But what video games most importantly give us is an unveiling of the blurred line between artist, art, and viewer.

William Shakespeare, whom I consider the <u>sage</u> of theater, repeatedly broke the fourth wall of his plays, a technique that we spoke about in chapter one. That invisible barrier separating the actors on <u>stage</u> from the audience dissipates to reveal a particular awareness on the part of the playwright from which both characters and viewers can benefit. My friend Firas Zreik who plays the *qanun* expresses that an artist is both talent and mission. This description fits Shakespeare perfectly.

> *"The novel is more of a whisper, whereas the stage is a shout."*
> – Robert Holman

But the Renaissance playwright did more than just break the fourth wall; he also tore down the fifth dimension separating viewers from the mirroring between the <u>world of the play</u> and the <u>play of the world</u>. The lines from *The Tempest* and *As You Like It* that we shared in the introductory chapter transcend a simple address from character to audience, both of which remain oblivious to the walls of the theater that imprison them. Indeed, "one man in his lifetime plays many parts" is no longer a <u>play</u>, but a <u>prayer</u>, <u>mediation</u>, and <u>meditation</u> on the <u>meaning</u> of existence.

Whereas <u>breaking</u> the fourth wall requires an actor to address their audience, while still in character, tearing the fifth wall involves <u>breathing</u> through the skin of illusion, <u>burning</u> the walls of "the globe theater itself" and finally being able to take one step away from the metaphor towards meaning. This is art at its highest level, where the mystical experience and creative process reveal themselves to be one and the same movement.

The great Greek tragedies like Antigone or Oedipus Rex and Shakespeare's plays or sonnets pave the way for us to reflect on the missive of filmmaking as more than creative endeavors, but also a mystical awakening of the highest order. Whereas on stage a character has the ability to directly address their audience, film and television is more subtle: it requires thespians who possess a magical power that can vicariously convey the glance of a character through the lens.

> *"Every time I go to a movie, it's magic, no matter what the movie's about."*
> – Steven Spielberg

The earliest memory of a movie I have is *Terminator 2: Judgement Day*, which I watched with my family multiple times, after the First Gulf War had destroyed Baghdad. We had already experienced judgment day prior to the film's release. There is one line, in the extended edition, where Sarah Connor exclaims at the end of the film: "The unknown future rolls towards us; I face it for the first time with a sense of hope. Because if a machine, the Terminator, can know the value of human life, maybe we can too."

And so, I did and still do. The judgment day of the First Gulf War did not leave behind so much hope. As we drove around the streets of Baghdad after that first night of bombing, we saw both buildings and people deformed with intestines and memories bloodily spilled on the streets. But it was *Terminator 2*, an action film that foretold some sort of resolution, that ultimately gifted us that hope. The glimmer of sacrifice is bestowed for the greater good. Such is the power of film as a medium for storytelling.

When I moved to Jordan with my family in 1992, another movie gave me solace after I left my homeland and tried to make new friends in a different country. *Edward Scissorhands* was not simply a film about a half-finished robot with scissors for hands, but a story about not fitting in a society that proclaims normalcy, while learning to appreciate what you are uniquely able to do that can create beauty in the world.

Edward, eloquently played by Johnny Depp, could have chosen to be a monster, a limit to which he was almost pushed by the 'real' monsters of suburbia. Instead, he took the path of seclusion and made ice sculptures that rained snow upon the people who once hurt him. The shards of ice descended on the residents below as a reminder that what allows us to create beauty can only manifest as such if it is embraced with harmony.

> *"As life progresses, images blur. All that remains are memories. Some of them true, some of them false."*
> – Dakota Fanning, *Brimstone*

For me, Edward espoused another sense of hope: my proverbial scissors with which I have to sculpt my story need not be used as people demand, rather for whatever the heart calls, even if that requires seclusion. Films like *Edward Scissorhands* and *Terminator 2: Judgment Day* continue to be markers of constancy in a world that is changing quickly. They provided me with solace during my childhood, but now I realize that it was also a safe space, like Edward's castle, where I could go and relate with the <u>familiar</u> when the world outside felt so <u>unfamilial</u>.

Another film that healed me immensely, from both war and diaspora, is Robert Downey Jr.'s *Heart and Soul*. As a young child, I saw myself in the young Thomas Reilly. Like him, I was also haunted by ghosts of deceased Iraqis, many of them my age, including the residents of shelter 25. Watching the story in this film unfold, where an adult Reilly helps each of the ghosts find peace, allowed me at the time to hope for some sort of redemption, for both me and those murdered.

As I discussed in the previous chapter on music, I did eventually find myself an adult Thomas Reilly. As I stood in front of a classroom and listened to Naseer Shamma play his piece commemorating the bombing of shelter 25, on that singular day in 2017 I managed to commune with the ghosts of Baghdad and found my own triumph and redemption. As Tom Hanks once tearfully expressed while reflecting on his masterpiece *Philadelphia*: "They last forever these movies!"

> *"If science fiction is the mythology of modern technology, then its myth is tragic."*
> – Ursula K. Le Guin

Now you might ask, but how do any of these examples demonstrate breaking the fourth or fifth wall? They are simply instances of a viewer being affected by a film they watched. My response here is that the deep aesthetic <u>sensibility</u> and <u>sensitivity</u> one can have while watching a play, tv show, or film is one of the best ways to tear down the veils separating art from life, thereby blurring the lines between actor, work, and viewer. This was the ancient purpose behind tragedies, dramas, and mythology generally.

We spoke about the modern temple known as 'museum' in a previous chapter; a building that was invented for citizens of the new world to visit and negotiate their identities. It is a mausoleum of shrines where, as

Cézanne instructs, beginning artists should go to find the spirit of their sage dormant in a painting or statue. The museum is but one of many ways in which our mythologies continue to live today, alongside film and theater.

As I am writing this chapter, the brilliant journalist Krista Tippett and her groundbreaking project, *On Being*, is helping produce a modern adaptation of a Greek classic: *Antigone in Savannah*. The reason for this, as the *On Being* website explains is because:

> It allows the timeless resonance of the ancient Greek texts to help us consider ourselves anew in history. *Antigone* poses searing questions that were pertinent in ancient Greece, have been pertinent throughout Georgia's history, and continue to be pertinent to all of us today. We are alive in a time of war, pestilence, and famine; some conditions of being human haven't changed in thousands of years. Yet in every period of history, amid troubling times, "human signposts" point us towards hope.

From Shakespeare to James Cameron's *Terminator 2* and this modern adaptation of *Antigone*, the message is clear: our human species needs stories and <u>words</u> to enchant an otherwise troubled and mundane <u>world</u>.

"I have never listened to anyone who criticized my taste in space travel, sideshows or gorillas. When this occurs, I pack up my dinosaurs and leave the room."
– Ray Bradbury, *Zen in the Art of Writing*

One of these sages of filmmaking, Steven Spielberg, is quoted above describing the magic he finds in every movie he watches. The director of *E.T.* and *Indiana Jones* is a perfect example of someone who seeks to provide hope in the world through the enchanting wizardry of filmmaking. In an interview, Spielberg discusses the wondrous experience he had entering a movie theater for the first time.

His father told him he would take him to see the 'greatest show on earth'. The young Spielberg believed this literally. When he entered the movie theater for the first time, he was amazed to find himself in what could only be described as a temple. The lined chairs that resembled pews in a church or synagogue and the elegant large curtain upfront all gave him the impression that he was at a place of worship.

Then, when the curtain opened and he saw the projector screen for the first time, in rolled the beginning of Cecil B. DeMille's *The Greatest Show on Earth*. From that moment onwards, Spielberg was ordained a filmmaker by both, his inner and external *lahut*. The countless train playing sets he had crashed, trying to reenact scenes from the movie, could best be described by him as "good ideas that always begin as bad ones. That is why it takes a long time."

"When you do comedy, you're not sitting at the grownups table, you're sitting at the children's table."
– Woody Allen

Undoubtedly, had young Spielberg not been allowed to reenact his passion with playsets, he would not have manifested his *lahut* in *E.T.*, *Close Encounters of the Third Kind*, *Jurassic Park*, *Indiana Jones*, *AI: Artificial Intelligence*, or countless other works. This is a return to the power of infancy: if children speak the language of spirits, I wonder how much we would deprive ourselves if we did not allow them to express their imagination?

What is also clear from Spielberg's journey as a filmmaker is that he tasted his craft at a young age by actually going to the movies. Quentin Tarantino expresses the same sentiment when he says: "When people ask me if I went to film school, I say: 'No, I went to films.'" This is an homage to what we discussed earlier on the journey towards the summit of the craft: no beginning artist is ever attracted and motivated to trek this mountain unless they are moved by works that reflect *haqiqa* (reality), not merely *shari'a* (law) or *tariqa* (path).

Or as Picasso instructed, to "learn the rules like an amateur, then break them like a pro." Spielberg and Tarantino had witnessed the *haqiqa* and *lahut* of their craft, an experience that continues to sustain them. Just as a single musical note can overwhelm volumes of poetry and oceans of prose, a single frame from the <u>reel</u> of <u>reality</u> can likewise suffice years of education. However, it never overthrows one's training and discipline, rather puts it in context and harmony with the larger <u>mission</u> and <u>missive</u> of art.

> *"Filmmaking is a chance to live many lifetimes."*
> – Robert Altman

Like Spielberg, my earliest memory of Baghdad before the war was also the movie theater. I must have watched my favorite childhood film, Tim Burton's *Batman* at least ten times in the showcase of the Mansour neighborhood. If Burton's *Edward Scissorhands* allowed me to cope as an outsider in neighboring Jordan and Robert Downy Jr's *Heart and Soul* gave me hope to commune with the ghosts of war, then *Batman* showed me what solace in darkness looks and feels like.

I am not only referring to the caped crusader himself or Burton's <u>gothic</u> adaptation of <u>Gotham</u>, but more importantly how the dark <u>knight's</u> own <u>night</u> permeated the inner hall of the temple showcase. The dance with the devil in the pale moonlight' between Batman and Joker, played by Michael Keaton and Jack Nicholson, showed me how the pain of loss can be turned into a sacrifice and, in turn, redemption. More importantly, these recurrent visits to the Mansour theater are an imprint in my memory of a better and more peaceful Baghdad.

It is remarkable that the darkness of Gotham, its heroes, and villains is luminous enough to cleanse the stygian night of Baghdad in my memory. But such is the power of film and cinema. Spielberg's experience watching *The Greatest Show on Earth* ushered his lifelong journey as a filmmaker, while my childhood at Mansour's showcase provided much-needed stability in a lifetime of migration and diaspora.

> *"Faithless is he that says farewell when the road darkens."*
> – J.R.R. Tolkien

Indeed, Spielberg's vision of the movie theater as a place of worship is not exaggerated. That is how I also remember the cinemas in my native homeland. In the *Power of Myth*, Joseph Campbell describes the transcendence he experienced when entering a cathedral in downtown Manhattan. He feels as though he had pierced a different dimension. Ironically, Campbell holds that we do not really have mythic places in modernity where temporality is reframed. I hope our journey thus far in this book allows us to rethink Campbell's view.

Of course, Campbell's mentorship helped birth one of the greatest sagas of our age, *Star Wars*. George Lucas, the creator of this universe was mentored by Campbell. In the series of interviews with Bill Moyers that were eventually transcribed and collected into the *Power of Myth* Moyers asks Campbell whether *Star Wars* follows the traditional myth. "It is all there!", he says. However, Lucas gives us a deeper insight into what inspired him to weave this myth.

The two main threads that inspire *Star Wars* are – on the one hand – belief and – on the other hand – fathers and sons. Moyers asks Lucas whether the world he created is about faith, to which Lucas responds: "It is less about faith and more so about God. I am more worried when I ask a young person on the street: 'do you believe in God?', and they answer: 'I don't know', than if they simply say: 'no'". Lucas is thoroughly invested in breaking the fourth and fifth walls of his work, hoping, like Shakespeare, that his audience is driven to ask the big questions.

"I was born by myself but carry the spirit and blood of my father, mother and my ancestors. So, I am really never alone. My identity is through that line."
– Ziggy Marley

In another interview, the creator of 'galaxies far away' states that his creation is ultimately about 'fathers and sons'. Anakin Skywalker emerges as a Christic figure who has no father, one that Lucas inundates with temptations and the 'dark side of the force.' Anakin is attracted to evil by a spiritual father figure, the Sith lord Palpatine. Luke, Anakin's son, is born as a redeemer who has to cleanse his father from Palpatine's influence, but who also finds himself in a similar position when his own nephew and disciple, Ben Solo, is drawn to the way of the Sith.

This network of suffering and redemption reaches its climax in Rey, Palpatine's granddaughter and Luke's disciple. In a powerful scene at the end of this saga, the spirits of all the Jedi grant her strength to face her grandfather and untie the knots of suffering that have plagued all sons and fathers in Lucas' universe, beginning with Anakin. This reminds us of the cumulative and gradual revelation of the *insan kamil tamm*, in stages that culminate in a symbiotic synthesis.

Anakin Skywalker, who was prophesied to be the 'one who will bring balance to the force', is unable to fulfill this role by himself. Instead, his mission is spread over various characters, beginning with himself and culminating with Rey. But let us not get distracted by the series of failures exhibited by the protagonists, because Lucas is subtly alluding to the power of genealogy here. In the final battle, when Palpatine faces Rey, he proclaims: "I am all the Sith", as she responds: "And I am all the Jedi."

> *"Our ancestors are totally essential to our every waking moment, although most of us don't even have the faintest idea about their lives, their trials, their hardships or challenges."*
> – Annie Lennox

'Fathers and sons' is a theme that predominates modern mythology. Aside from *Star Wars*, in J.R.R. Tolkien's masterpieces *The Hobbit* and *Lord of the Rings* one finds a similar weaving of genealogy that ties knots of suffering, then unties them with redemption. Aragorn, the promised king of Middle Earth is tasked with redeeming the line of Isildur, his ancestor who was tempted by the ring of power. The wizard Gandalf must likewise cleanse his order of dark temptations by facing his master – a spiritual father – Saruman the White.

In a powerful scene in the *Two Towers*, Gandalf returns after passing his rites of passage and defeating the Balrog of Morgoth as Gandalf the White. When Aragorn proclaims upon seeing the reborn wizard: "Forgive me, I thought you were Saruman", he responds: "But I am Saruman, or Saruman as he should have been." As the Qur'an states: "If you turn away [from your path], He will exchange you with others who will be unlike you" (47:38). Saruman had not fulfilled the role destined for his archetype. Thus, he was exchanged by another white wizard, his own disciple Gandalf.

We likewise find Frodo Baggins who undertakes the journey of destroying the ring of power to redeem the faults of his uncle and caretaker Bilbo. Even the latter himself was only coaxed by Gandalf out of the Shire and onto an adventure to steal the Arkenstone from the dragon Smaug when the wizard reminded him of the courage of his grandfather Bandobras Took, the 'Bullroarer'. At the end of the saga, Frodo delegates his journey to his companion, Samwise Gamgee. The ring of power could only be destroyed through these series of lineaged sufferings and redemptions.

"Our religion is the traditions of our ancestors - the dreams of our old men, given them in solemn hours of the night by the Great Spirit; and the visions of our sachems, and is written in the hearts of our people."
– Chief Seattle

We find the same overarching genealogy in the world of superheroes, including the two universes of Marvel and DC Comics. Perhaps the most well-known example is Gotham's caped crusader Batman, whose inner demons and outer quest for vengeance was <u>born</u> after his parents' <u>death</u>. In a poignant scene in the recent film *Batman vs. Superman*, Clark Kent mumbles the name Martha, Bruce Wayne's mother, as he is beaten by Batman. The latter becomes furious when Superman mentions his mother's name, only to find out from Lois that Martha also happens to be the name of Kent's adoptive mother.

Gandalf and Saruman, Rey and Anakin, Aragorn and Isildur, Batman and Superman, these are all instances of archetypes that contend with one another, producing self-knowledge in characters, actors, and audience. This much is mentioned in the Qur'an clearly: "Had God not coerced people, one against the other, then earth would have gone to corruption" (2:251). Likewise, in the TV show *Titans*, mentioned in previous chapters, all the heroes must deal with their genealogies, where parents are either missing and must be <u>replaced</u> or evil and need to be <u>redeemed</u>.

> *"If you want a happy ending, that depends of course on where you want to stop your story."*
> – Orson Welles

Ibn al-'Arabi has much to teach us about contentions between fathers and sons. Beginning with the verse mentioned in the previous paragraph, the Sufi mystic explores another statement in the Qur'an: "The example of a good Word is like a good *shajarah* [tree], its roots are firm in the ground while its branches are high in the sky. It bears fruits at all times" (14:24). He creatively connects the word *shajarah* with *mushajarah* (<u>contention</u>), <u>contending</u> that quarrels are a natural course in life through which light and <u>contentment</u> can spread, while darkness expires.

This harmonizes with his maxim that we've revisited often: "Reality is perplexity, perplexity is anxiety and movement, and movement is life." Friction and contention are one of the many ways through which movement thrives in the universe. And beings are <u>made</u> to <u>move</u>, Ibn al-'Arabi tells us, when they're in love and searching for the beloved. All are incessantly marching towards their *mustaqarr* (place of stillness), like the sun. The Sufi mystic also told us about the poets who annihilate their words seeking existent things (e.g., status, women, wealth), not realizing the singular hidden treasure that resides behind these *suwar* (forms). Likewise, the characters in our mythologies are searching for their *lahut*. Their orbits cross and sometime collide. In the end, truth and reality emerge in the least likely of places.

"There is beauty in our roots. Sometimes we think our roots are shameful, and people tell you that you're no good or your ancestors are no good or that you come from a neighborhood of no hope and terrible crime. But it's about the beauty of those places, and I carry that with me."
– Luis Alberto Urrea

Regarding fathers and sons, Ibn al-ʿArabi describes the relationship between the first prophet Adam and his descendant the later prophet David. While discussing the creation of Adam, God informs the angels: "I am making a deputy upon the earth". However, the Sufi mystic insists that the deputy here is not actually this first prophet, but his descendant David. The proof can be found in another verse: "Oh David, We are making you a deputy upon the earth." Of course, it is the prophet Muhammad ﷺ who is the perfect and complete human and culmination of all potentialities and stations of previous prophets, including *khilafa* (deputyship).

In the Qurʾan, Moses accompanies the sage Khidr as the latter teaches him about the superiority of *haqiqa* (spiritual reality) above *shariʿa* (law). In one instance, the saint builds a wall to cover a treasure. When Moses asks him about the reason, Khidr explains that the treasure belonged to two orphans, and he feared it would be stolen. He also remarks that the orphans' 7th grandfather was a righteous man, hence God wanted them to receive this treasure for his sake.

Ibn al-ʿArabi revisits genealogy during his spiritual ascension. In the 7th heaven he meets prophet Abraham who instructs him to hold on to the 'brotherhood of milk'. The Sufi mystic deciphers this as a reference to a genealogy born through knowledge. Unsurprisingly, as mentioned, the prophet ﷺ had interpreted the vision of milk in both dreams and wakefulness as an allusion to knowledge. There are other genealogies that can be <u>formed</u> and <u>forged</u> besides that of blood, some of them might even substitute the absence of biological parents.

The artist Tanya Aguiñiga from Tijuana talks about the fascinating notion of 'crafting lineage'. As an immigrant living in San Diego, she highlights that the masters of her craft emerge as chains in a spiritual genealogy that remedies the absence of biological ancestors. She might not know her great grandfather but can recount the entire lineage of her teachers back to some meaningful origin. Art not only allows us to create imaginal ancestries in stories, but also weave our own as artists. Most importantly, in both cases, the end result is redemptive and healing.

> *"We forget that the soul has its own ancestors."*
> – James Hillman

Anakin was prophesied to bring balance to the force yet was not destined to do so. Nevertheless, this potential was dormant within him and passed on to his son Luke, and later Rey who fulfilled that prophecy. Likewise, The station of deputyship was initiated in the prophet Adam, but it was not meant to manifest outwardly until much later, in the prophet David. Finally, it culminated in the prophet of Islam. This is a recurring healing promise in all myths: start the work, but do not be discouraged by the prospect that the result might not manifest through you. Have the conviction that the tree you plant will <u>bear</u> its fruits, and these will <u>bear</u> your mark.

Bringing film and theater together, a transformative moment in my life that heightened my appreciation for this artform was a documentary I had watched in high school, *Looking for Richard.* My English teacher and mentor Ryan Goble had shown us the work in order to better understand the multiple literary layers animating one of Shakespeare's best plays, *Richard III.* However, this documentary did more than elaborate the world of the play itself but also illuminated, through the medium of film, the creative process of acting.

> *"When you reach the top, that's when the climb begins."*
> – Sir Michael Caine

A sage of his craft, Al Pacino is the 'protagonist' of this documentary. He takes the viewer on a journey to discover the difficulties American actors have playing Shakespeare. He interviews various British masters of theater, such as Sir John Gielgud, to ask them about the difficulty capable actors from across the ocean have in bringing Shakespeare's world to life. What impressed me most about the documentary is the subtle lens of the camera that paradoxically augments the power of theater.

We reminisce here on Jack Lemon's prerogative to keep doing less until one does nothing; that ideal meditation at the summit of art. Sir Michael Caine, who recounts this story, gives another demonstration using a camera closeup. Whereas on stage, an actor would have to physically move in order to address different characters or show the audience that focus has switched from one part of the world of the play to another, that is hardly the case on film.

"Indeed, Our command is like the blink of an eye" (54:50). Caine shows that all it takes is one glance on camera for the audience to notice that something has changed. A new character has entered the screen, perhaps another has left. Whatever the case, the camera's power is a poignant manifestation of two divine names that are – unsurprisingly – anagrams: *Qarib* (Near) and *Raqib* (Watchful).

> *"A number of images put a certain way become something quite above and beyond what any of them are individually."*
> – Francis Ford Coppola

In *Looking for Richard*, the camera humbles the actors' grandiose performance. More than that, the craft of film itself emerges as the breaking of the fourth and fifth walls of theater. It is a spectacle that Shakespeare could have only dreamed of. And yet, it takes a capable sage like Pacino to know how to utilize this interlaced layering of visions. In one scene, he speaks to the camera as himself, while in another he walks hunchback through an archway in modern London, completely transformed to Richard. He blurs world and play between the opening: "now is the winter of our discontent" and informing viewers that he secretly plans to kill the widow lady Anne: "I will not keep her for long."

In *The Godfather Part II*'s last breath, when Michael Corleone's daughter is shot and killed, Al Pacino brings his mastery of theater to the <u>scene</u> on <u>screen</u> and wails for what seems like an eternity. It is a dramatization that takes the breath out of my body and soul every time I watch it. However,

I was surprised when I listened to Pacino explain that his wailing was not a single shot, but multiple ones that were brilliantly threaded on film.

In another documentary, *Derrida* about the French philosopher who accompanies us in this book, the protagonist shows viewers that prior to agreeing to do the documentary, he had interlaced an intricate web of mirrors by filming himself, then filming himself watching that, and so on and so forth. His fright and critique of the camera is not unfounded. In the first few minutes, he is accompanied by the camera man on the street. The latter trips and almost falls, at which Derrida smiles and wonders: "How amazing that you're the one with the camera, yet blind!"

"I believe that in a great city, or even in a small city or a village, a great theatre is the outward and visible sign of an inward and probable culture."
– Laurence Olivier

In many ways, theater is a mirror of the Sufi *hadra* (presence), an ecstatic dance that begins from stillness and reaches the climactic ʿ*amar* (construction). It is a performance that seeks to presence the *lahut* in the center. The interactivity between audience and dancers, celestial-like movements, sounds that are larger than life, and the need to tear down the invisible walls for higher communication to take place are all movements that highlight the stages of Sufi practices and drama as one and the same.

Film, on the other hand, is as the sage Martin Scorsese has eloquently defined cinema, as a "matter of what is in the frame and what is out." The camera deceives us. Fortunately, it is often for our own sake. Whereas the stage was always meant to be the ascension platform towards the external *lahut*, film I feel takes us inwardly. Like a musical instrument, it forces one to be <u>silent</u> and <u>listen</u>. And just when we think we have reached the ocean bed of stillness, the ground gives below us to reveal yet another destination.

Like Jack Lemon, actors in front of the camera, and all of us who play many parts in life, we are challenged to do less. And then, when we think we have reached the summit, there is Sir Michael Caine to tell us that now we must start climbing. The camera, this reflective mirror of the *Raqib/Qarib* (Watchful Near) is catching every glance, emotion, and memory. It <u>returns</u> and <u>reflects</u> back to us our truths and lies.

While commenting on the brilliance of the composer John Williams, Steven Spielberg says that his friend's countless scores have not only enhanced his films, but actually tell the story. The melody is what unlocks meaning, as we have learned in the last chapter. On film, all the artforms come together. They need not work in harmony, but nevertheless struggle to do so in order to show us how we can do that in our own lives. The beautiful paradox of our species is that we can express our collective *mustaqarr* (place of stillness) beautifully in <u>reelity</u>, despite our inability to do that often in <u>reality</u>.

Ma'rifa and *'Urf*: On Society and Mythology

"I alone cannot change the world, but I can cast a stone across the water to create many ripples."
– Mother Teresa

In the Qur'an, the quest for gnosis is tied to community and society: "Oh people, We have created you from male and female and made you into nations and tribes *lita'arafu* [so that you may come to know one another]" (49:13). The term used in this verse *lita'arafu* is from the same root as *ma'rifa* (gnosis). We have seen it before while discussing the Sufi teaching: "Whoever knows him/herself will know their Lord", and Ibn al-'Arabi's reformulation: "Whoever knows him/herself, he/she has already known their Lord."

The Qur'an highlights another related term, *'urf* (custom) and its importance: "Take the path of forgiveness and command *'urf*" (7:199). These two verses, along with this Sufi teaching, reveal the layers of meaning pertaining to inner spiritual knowledge and the importance of society as the stage where collective imagination unfolds. As we have learned, from self-knowledge of the individual to community, the microcosm <u>reflects</u> and <u>refracts</u> the macrocosm and metacosm.

Ibn al-'Arabi also distinguishes between two forms of knowing: *ma'rifa* (esoteric gnosis) and *'ilm* (exoteric knowledge). The network of words that are etymologically related to the second term include: *'alama* (signpost), *'alam* (world), and *'alim* (knower). He states the reason the world is called *'alam* is because it is a matrix of signs that allude to the *'alim* (knower) who is God. This pays homage to the linguistic connections that, for Ibn al-'Arabi, are a window into metaphysical relationships.

> *"In the midst of winter, I find within me the invisible summer."*
> – Leo Tolstoy, *The Kingdom of God is Within You*

Since both *'ilm* and *ma'rifa* have an external macrocosmic and social dimension, how can we distinguish between them? In other words, what does it mean to have *'ilm* (exoteric knowledge) of one's community and how is that different from *ma'rifa* (esoteric gnosis) of the same people? For Ibn al-'Arabi, these two wings of knowing are not exclusive. Rather, they overlap and complement one another.

Here, we need refer back to al-Junayd's definition of gnosis: "The color of water is the color of the cup," which is central to understanding how *'ilm* and *ma'rifa* dance together in Ibn al-'Arabi's harmonious vision between microcosm and macrocosm. We can only know our immediate and distant surroundings according to our inner *lahut* and hidden treasure. And so, who we are ultimately shapes the world we perceive. This is the underlying reality of the divine statement mentioned previously: "I am at My servant's opinion of me. So let them think of Me well."

For Ibn al-ʿArabi, *ʿilm* comes neither before nor after *maʿrifa*; they constantly sustain one another. To have *ʿilm* of anything external to us (e.g., tree, rock, building, human beings) is to decipher the <u>ode</u> of their inner *lahut* and hidden treasure from the <u>code</u> of their *nasut*. For two reasons, this allows us to have better *maʿrifa* of ourselves. First, we are one of the beings who inhabit the universe and secondly, the color and shape of our cup determines the *ʿilm* we receive.

"Humans are vulnerable and rely on the kindnesses of the earth and the sun; we exist together in a sacred field of meaning."
– Joy Harjo

And so, as we learn and engage with our immediate culture, we are ourselves changing and adapting, which in turn shapes how we continue to perceive the world. However, the metaphysical lens that Ibn al-ʿArabi adds to this framework is how to better understand the spiritual significance of culture. What importance do films, music, plays, literature, and architecture have in a particular community? Aside from entertaining us, what else they voice?

If the art we each produce is the missive from a hidden treasure, our inner *lahut*, then the collective imagination of a community is likewise communication from the macrocosmic heart and center of society. This is precisely why God instructs the prophet ﷺ to command *ʿurf* (custom)', because that is the macrocosmic *maʿrifa* (esoteric knowledge). In other words, the *'urf* of a community is the description of its inner cup: its shape, size, and color.

Continuing with this thread, and returning to our previous comparison between prose and poetry, I would like to juxtapose this contrast on both microcosmic and macrocosmic levels: just as the human body is our exoteric grammar and prose, while the spirit is our esoteric poetry, so are the laws and disciplines that govern the physical lives of any society its exoteric body and prose, whereas the humanities and arts are their collective esoteric spirit and poetry.

> *"We don't read and write poetry because it's cute. We read and write poetry because we are members of the human race. And the human race is filled with passion. And medicine, law, business, engineering, these are noble pursuits and necessary to sustain life. But poetry, beauty, romance, love, these are what we stay alive for."*
> – Robin Williams, *Dead Poets Society*

This vision is beautifully described in the Qur'anic story of Moses. In chapter 14, one finds an introductory verse just prior to returning to the story of this prophet: "We have not sent a messenger save in the tongue of his people, so that he can clarify for them" (14:4). The following verse continues: "And We have sent Moses with our signs: 'Take your people from the darkness to the light, and remind them of the days of God. Indeed in this are signs for every patient and grateful person'" (14:5).

The first verse, a preamble to the story of Moses in this chapter of scripture, provides an insight into the role of language and eloquence in this prophet's mission. When God tells Moses to speak to pharaoh, the former asks: "Oh my Lord, expand my chest for me, facilitate my affair, and untie the knot from my tongue, so that they may understand my speech. And give me a helper from my family, my brother Aaron. Strengthen me through him and make him my partner in this affair" (20:25-32).

Even though Moses asks God to 'untie the knot from his tongue, so that they may understand his speech', in reference to the fact that oration might not be his strength, in another verse he clarifies why his brother Aaron is a necessary companion in this mission: "And my brother Aaron, for he is more eloquent than me in tongue" (28:34). In other words, Moses felt that the ability to simply speak using the same grammar as Pharaoh is not sufficient, one also needs to master the 'cultural tongue' of eloquence; to be able to speak directly to people's hearts and their inner poetry.

> *"Eloquence is a painting of the thoughts."*
> – Blaise Pascal

Let us remember that <u>eloquence</u> in Arabic, *balagha* – also known as *bayan*, a term that has the added meaning of '<u>proclamation</u>' – was defined by the palestinian poet and father of oudist Ahmad al-Khatib as the ability to precisely convey a thought in as few words as possible while leaving no doubt in the mind and heart of the listener as to the intended meaning. It is a relationship between the *nafis* (precious) meanings that reside in the *nafs* (soul), pertaining to our inner microcosmic *ma'rifa*, and how they are <u>perceived</u> and <u>received</u> by others who collectively form the macrocosmic *'urf* (custom).

It is for this reason that Moses sought Aaron as a companion, not merely so that Pharaoh can understand the prophet's mission, but more so that it can be expressed in the best way possible, using terms and references that are unique to the minds and hearts of the people at the time. This is ultimately what eloquence is: a present and relevant awareness of what a people are feeling inclined towards or despised of; to appreciate and acknolwedge that, to regard it as sacred and a part of our calling.

I once read an amazing story from the life of the prophet ﷺ to this effect. After the spread of Islam, during a year known as the year of delegations, countless tribes came from across Arabia to declare their Islam. One of them hailed from a region that spoke a very difficult dialect of Arabic that no other tribe knew or understood. They were also known for brewing wine by placing grape juice in wooden cups made from the bark of palm trees. They would leave the drink in these cups for some time until it ferments.

"Do you ever get the feeling people are incapable of not caring? People are amazing."
– Brendan Frasier, *The Whale*

This tribe also had specific names for these drinks in their dialect. It should be made clear that, at this point in time, Islam had already forbidden alcohol; it was a commonly known censure among Muslims. And yet, when this tribe entered into the court of the prophet ﷺ he greeted and called them by none other than the names of these drinks. I often tell students in my retreats: "Imagine how scandalous it would be in the eyes of Muslims today if their preacher at a mosque welcomed non-Muslim guests by saying: 'Welcome to the people of budweiser, whiskey, and champagne!'"

And yet, this is exactly how the prophet of Islam greeted this delegation; a gesture that immediately won their hearts, and they embraced Islam. The only request the prophet ﷺ made of them is to drink the grape juice without allowing it to ferment in the wooden cups, thereby not forbidding it completely. The tribe returned some months later and complained that it was too difficult for them to drink the juice without fermentation, since it had been a tradition they inherited for many generations.

"Eloquence, at its highest pitch, leaves little room for reason or reflection, but addresses itself entirely to the desires and affections, captivating the willing hearers, and subduing their understanding."
– David Hume

Acknowledging their failed attempt at 'prohibition', the prophet ﷺ instructed them to wean themselves gradually, by slowly reducing the amount of time this drink remains in wooden cups, until they are able to consume it without any fermentation at all. If we look at this story through the lens of metaphysics, the prophet's wisdom here is not simply a matter of respecting people's tradition and culture. Instead, Ibn al-ʿArabi focuses on the prophet's divinely gifted status of having *jawamiʿ al-kalim* (all encompassing speech).

We have already delved into the significance of *kalima* (word) and *kalam* (speech) to appreciate this prophetic title. Historically, it refers to him as the *insan kamil tamm* (perfect and complete human) who is the cumulative synthesis of all prior divine prophetic *kalimat* (Words), from Adam to Jesus. But more than that, it also highlights his divinely-ordained ability to address each individual and community according to their hidden treasure and *lahut*.

And this should be our destination as well as we reflect on our place in society and our ability to contribute to the collective consciousness. To return to *'ilm* and *ma'rifa* in society, it is not enough to just add art to the gamut of what is being produced and consumed, but first to recognize that what exists in culture is already the *'urf* of the macrocosmic hidden treasure. It necessarily bares the mark of divine wisdom and the Sacred. Otherwise, it would not exist.

> *"The arts and humanities are vastly more important in troubled times."*
> – Jim Leach

I would like to add one final point to further emphasize the sanctity of culture, both its beauty and ugliness. Here is another mirroring between the individual (microcosm) and community (macrocosm). In Islamic eschatology, the discipline pertaining to the end of days, there are three moments of death: the minor hour which describes the passing of an individual, the major hour or death of all humanity, and in-between them the middle hour that concerns the passing of a community or civilization.

This poignantly places society as the *barzakh* (liminal threshold) and – in turn – imaginal realm connecting a person to all of humanity. It is a perplexing and paradoxical <u>space</u> where, as we learned, contentions take <u>place</u>. However, in the end, fruits grow and the good tree rises to heaven. The branches of this *shajarah* that continue to live and thrive, even after a community passes, are their arts. Hence, we still find today the *Odyssey*, *Aeneid*, Plato's *Republic*, epic of *Gilgamish*, and traces of precious *anfas* (breaths) from the past that immortalize the *nafis* (precious) hidden treasures of a people.

I am reminded here of an episode in *Star Trek: The Next Generation* when captain Jean-Luc Picard faints after a probe drifting in space tethered itself to his mind. We find him living a vision as a married man on a planet. He has a wife to whom he tries to explain that he is a captain of a ship who found himself on their planet by mistake. It takes many months to convince him otherwise, but in this dream world, he finally believes that this is home.

He begets children and learns to play the flute. As he continues to live in this imaginal world, he learns that the planet is dying of drought. He aids his family and friends in building a probe to launch into space and search for help. After his – dream – wife dies and children grow older, at 80 years old his daughter takes him to the town square for the launching of the probe. There, he finds his deceased wife and friends back to bid him farewell from his imaginal journey. They tell him that they had already died thousands of years ago, and this vision is their only chance at remembrance: "Keep our memory alive."

> *"Faced with collective forgetting, we must strive to remember."*
> – Reni Eddo-Lodge

Picard awakens on his ship and finds that the 80 years he had spent on that planet were merely 18 minutes in the 'real' world. The most remarkable moment in this episode is when the probe was opened and a small box containing a flute was found inside. Picard, a character played brilliantly by Sir Patrick Stewart, holds the instrument close to his heart then <u>prays</u> it like a maestro who learned how to <u>play</u> in a dream. The connections abound here, perhaps most vivid among which are two phrases, "keep our memory alive", as I was told by the ghosts of shelter 25 and the oppressed at the Island of Gorée, and "we are such stuff as dreams are made on, and our little life is rounded with a sleep."

One finds a similar story in the teachings of ʿAbdul ʿAziz al-Dabbagh, who speaks of a man that lived in Baghdad with family and children. One day, he made ablution in the Euphrates, only to find himself after washing his face in a completely different land unknown to him. After becoming accustomed to his new setting, he marries another woman and begets new children. Years later, he returns to the river to wash his face, and finds himself again in his native Baghdad. No time had passed in between.

> *"Translation is not a matter of words only: it is a matter of making intelligible a whole culture."*
> – Anthony Burgess

I would like to transition to a liminal topic, pertaining to the sanctity of creativity and how we can metaphysically distinguish between high and low art. This is a rather <u>controversial</u> and <u>convoluted</u> topic for many religious people, many of whom ask me: "If all art is coming from our hidden treasure, then how do we account for drugs, sex, and violence in films, music, and video games?" Here, we need to return to our definition of the creative process as a translation of the ineffable into the tangible.

Ibn al-ʿArabi is explicitly clear about the ultimate source of human imagination: "Every human being, if and when they imagine, then their perception extends to divine imagination." Notice how the Sufi mystic universalizes his statement so that it encompasses all people regardless of faith. Anybody who imagines and translates their vision into a novel, poem, song, sculpture, building, or video game is receiving – at the source – directly from divine imagination.

This is the true sense of *tawhid* (oneness), a central pillar in Islam. Unlike its commonly understood definition, 'believing God is one', Ibn al-ʿArabi understands *tawhid* in its literal sense: to perceive or make oneness in all things. In the case of human creativity, this means to root all the diverse manifestations of art in the metacosmic *lahut*. This is also expressed in another Sufi teaching: "In everything is a sign that He is one."

> *"The translation called good has original value as a work of art."*
> – Benedetto Croce

If some of us cannot <u>perceive</u> those signs, it does not imply that they do not exist, only that we are unable to <u>receive</u> them due to a dissonance between them and our dispositions. Either way, what is important here is the process whereby the initial inspiration in the hidden treasure is translated into an external work of art, per the five levels of being and the creative process we discussed in chapter two. And yet, how can we decipher a divine origin in works that belie such a description?

First, what does it even mean to say that a work of art is profane? According to which standard is that the case? For a novel that praises the trinity will be seen as sacrligious by a Muslim, while a poem that celebrates paganism will be regarded as heretical by many adherents to all three monotheisms. In general, art should first and foremost be understood in the context of its own *ʿilm* and *ʿurf*, not according to the dispositions of its viewers.

But let us be honest, what about a can of excrement at a museum. How can that be considered art of divine origin? It is here that we must take into account the fragility of the translation process, from conception to birth. This journey goes through many stages and buffers, including disposition, natural and social conditioning, ego and what we call today 'inner demons'. What might imprint itself in the essence of an artist as a fragrant rose could very well be born as a deaf thorn, due to years of oppression and trauma.

"I don't make a particular distinction between 'high art' and 'low art.' Music is there for everybody. It's a river we can all put our cups into and drink it and be sustained by it."
– John Williams

And this is why we continue to ask the important question of any display of creativity: what is the artist trying to say, and how does that manifest? This is neither a question that everybody can answer about all art nor is it easy to address at all times. Not every poem will make sense to all of us. Luckily, there is enough art to suffice all of humanity. But sincerely, instead of focusing on bad art, why not linger on that which speaks to your inner *lahut* and in which you feel invested enough to seek the answer to this question: what is the artist trying to tell me?

Jim Cornette, a brilliant storyteller in the world of professional wrestling, once gave this eloquent criticism of the overuse of violence in this form of entertainment: "It desensitizes an audience, whereby we could no longer use a chair shot or blood meaningfully as a climactic point in a story. This is the problem with extreme wrestling." I would venture to say that all religious scriptures contain violence, and so it must be in art as well. The question is what purpose does it serve in the story? Does it <u>dilute</u> the narrative or <u>delude</u> the audience? In this case, the <u>abscess</u> of violence is as harmful as its <u>absence</u>.

We <u>transition</u> now to the macrocosmic creative process, the journey of <u>translation</u> whereby a community renders its deepest spiritual sensibilities into cultural *'urf* and art. I began contemplating this question after realizing a trend in the American Muslim community of criticizing the widespread English renditions of Rumi's poetry, most auspiciously by Coleman Barks. The common argument against these translations is: "The West is taking Islam out of Rumi."

> *"Culture is the arts elevated to a set of beliefs."*
> – Thomas Wolfe

And yet, it is American Muslims themselves who have long since "taken Rumi out of Islam." He cannot be found in the curriculum of any Islamic seminary in North America, nor will that change once the ongoing 'authentic translation' project is completed and widely available. This is because the problem is not Barks' supposed mistranslation of Rumi's poetry, but rather the widespread misunderstanding of how spiritual traditions travel from their intellectual homeland to new frontiers in the collective imagination.

When we investigate the greatest cultural epics of our time, such as *Star Wars*, *Lord of the Rings*, *Harry Potter*, *Marvel*, and *DC Comics* we find at their source the teachings of some ancient tradition. As mentioned, George Lucas was mentored by Joseph Campbell, the author of *The Power of Myth*, a book that is itself a study of ancient mythology. Likewise, both Tolkien and Rowling <u>adopted</u> and <u>adapted</u> their passionate faith in Christianity to varying degrees in the worlds of Middle Earth and Hogwarts, respectively.

Putting aside all the 'superficial' accusations of witchcraft against *Harry Potter*, who would in their right mind say that the story is actually a mistranslation of Christianity? Art is not meant to be a literal translation of an original meaning, rather as Ibn al-ʿArabi instructs us to do with everything in this world, it is a *taʿbir* (interpretation). The collective cultural consciousness is not – nor should it be – <u>concerned</u> with any theological or technical <u>concepts</u> in Rumi's poetry, only that a rendition speaks from the summit.

"Woe to the makers of literal translations, who by rendering every word weaken the meaning! It is indeed by so doing that we can say the letter kills and the spirit gives life."
– Voltaire

"Speak to people *ʿala qadri ʿuqulihim* [according to how they understand]". This teaching by the prophet ﷺ is often used by many Muslim teachers as an excuse to not delve into metaphysics, of the kind that we have discussed in this book, lest people misunderstand it. However, I offer here a modified translation that focuses not on the content, grammar, or body of what is being spoken, but the method in which it is conveyed. This is the 'cultural tongue' that God commanded and for which purpose Moses requested the aid of his brother Aaron.

And so, in the case of Rumi's poetry and the Sufi tradition generally, there does indeed to be an 'authentic' translation, in the sense that it closely reflects the theological and legalistic objectives of Rumi himself. However, such a rendition is proper only for Muslims, not the general populace. Its purpose would be for readers devoted to the Islamic tradition to become better Muslims in the strictest sense, but not for an atheist businessman on Wall Street to be able to live a better life.

Rumi himself says in his *Mathnawi*: "There is a field beyond belief and unbelief, I will meet you there." As T.S. Eliot also expresses: "The intersection of the timeless with time, that is an occupation for the saint." The *'urf* of culture is the intersection of countless dispositions, hidden treasures and instances of the microcosmic inner *lāhūt*. The only way to address all souls at once is through the prism of *jawāmiʿ al-kalim*, the perfect and complete man, whereby the address is not from <u>ear</u> to <u>ear</u>, but <u>heart</u> to <u>heart</u>.

"You may possess only a small light, but uncover it, let it shine, use it in order to bring more light and understanding to the hearts and minds of men and women. Give them, not hell, but hope and courage. Do not push them deeper into their theological despair but preach the kindness and everlasting love of God."
– Alfred S. Cole

Thenceforth, as the 'authentic' translation of Rumi's poetry circulates among his coreligionists, there needs to be outsiders that act as mediators who will not engage with the work in its original language, in this case <u>Persian</u>, but rather a <u>version</u> closer to their own register. Coleman Barks does not know Persian and never read the original *Mathnawi*. Rather, he engaged with Reynold Nicholson's more academic translation. Had Barks actually read an 'authentic' rendition, intended for a Muslim audience, he might not have been moved to interpret the Sufi mystic's poetry at all.

Unfortunately, some Muslim readers might suppose such a prospect to be a great idea. However, let us contemplate the fact that because of Coleman Barks, the name Rumi was mentioned numerous times on talk shows, musical albums, and published books across America. I was incredibly humbled once while reading Gerard Elmore's translation of Ibn al-'Arabi's *The Fabulous Gryphon*. In the introduction, Elmore says that his mere affiliation with a saint of God through this project is an honor that he hopes might be a source for salvation on the Day of Judgment.

The American Muslim community should be less concerned that Rumi is understood correctly – yes, I mean that – and more so that his name is on every tongue, that he provides some sort of solace for people in every minor and major difficulty they are facing. Yes, that includes someone breaking up with their boy or girlfriend. No manifestation of loss or separation is insignificant; it all matters, if we are to correctly understand Ibn al-'Arabi's statement about poets and human beings who extinguish their words in love of existent things.

"If you have been in the vicinity of the sacred - ever brushed against the holy - you retain it more in your bones than in your head; and if you haven't, no description of the experience will ever be satisfactory."
– Daniel Taylor, *In Search of Sacred Places*

Before concluding this chapter on a more concrete pedagogical vision, I would like to linger for a moment on the notion of collective memory. The Sufi sage Shaykh Hisham Kabbani states that when God first created the different continents, He ordered the holy spirit Gabriel to place a sacred stone in each of these landmasses that contains the *ma'arif* (pl. *ma'rifa*) specific to the people of that land. The same holy spirit that had cast the

Word of God to Mary also – literally – set in stone the Word that would become the hidden treasure of every community on earth.

Everywhere in the world, one finds such a stone that has some spiritual significance to its people: the black stone in Mecca, Dome of the Rock, and the Temple Mount in Jerusalem. Even in America, I had the honor of visiting one such large stone formation sacred to the indigenous native Americans in the city of Mahwah in New Jersey. It is a portal that opens a channel directly connecting our *nasut* to *lahut*. This is our Parthenon and Mount Olympus. This is the stage where mythologies are <u>formed</u> and beliefs <u>reformed</u>.

"I was standing on the highest mountain of them all, and round about beneath me was the whole hoop of the world. And while I stood there, I saw more than I can tell and I understood more than I saw; for I was seeing in a sacred manner the shapes of all things in the spirit, and the shape of all shapes as they must live together like one being. And I saw that the sacred hoop of my people was one of many hoops that made one circle, wide as daylight and as starlight, and in the center grew one mighty flowering tree to shelter all children of one mother and one father. And I saw that it was holy."
– Black Elk

The significance of both, these sacred stones and the myths that emerge from within and sustain them is like the walls of my home in Iraq: they chronicle the <u>memories</u> of a people in its crevices, as well as set the frontier for their <u>remembrance</u>. Each unfolding chapter of these narratives becomes an imprint in the heart of the community, another color and shape adjustment in the cup of their collective imagination and consciousness.

In America, this story is well-documented. The sages of native Americans perceived the Creator who sanctified a nature immersed in sacredness. This vision colored their rituals, dances, and way of life. The suffering and massacres they experienced at the hands of colonial Europeans continue to 'beautifully haunt' the land: their bodies murdered, while their spirits triumphantly become the earth's custodians. Like their sacred stones, the spirits of chiefs and their descendants today are portals for *lahut* to communicate with *nasut* in America.

And this must necessarily manifest through the arts, the most pristine manifestation of the collective hidden treasure. Creativity is how a community documents its suffering, often not realizing that the ability to tell one's story is itself the much-awaited redemption. And this we see as well with the oppressed and enslaved Africans who were ripped from their homeland and brought to America. Their suffering imprints itself in Jazz, Blues, HipHop and the spirituals through which they continue to both metaphorically and literally triumph against tyrants.

"Armed with the knowledge of our past, we can with confidence charter a course for our future. Culture is an indispensable weapon in the freedom struggle. We must take hold of it and forge the future with the past."
– Malcolm X

These cumulative imprints form a symbiotic whole that collectively shapes the *ʿurf* of the land. Any group that seeks to contribute to this vision, such as the immigrant Muslim community, must first understand and acknowledge this *ʿurf* and its sacredness. Not only that, but *idhn* (permission) must be actively sought from the sages of the land, while attentively lending them one's *udhun* (ear). In other words, be silent and listen.

I am a Sufi Muslim who is passionate about the beauty of Islamic mysticism and its ability to contribute and augment the already sacred spirit of America; a vision I hope this book has demonstrated. In turn, I am firmly convinced that Islamic seminaries in America need to envision their curriculums as a continuum from the foundational catechisms in the faith, including the Qur'an and prophetic teachings, all the way to contemporary popular culture.

But this translation from the Qur'an to Batman has to take place through meaningful mediations, the most indispensable among which is the metaphysical prism of Sufism through the lens of Sufi sages like Ibn al-ʿArabi. In every place in the world where the arts have thrived in a Muslim land, from Senegal to China, one finds at the source the liminal mediation of saints and their teachings. As long as Ibn al-ʿArabi's *The Meccan Openings* and *Bezels of Wisdom* or Rumi's *Mathnawi* are not part of the educational equation, there can be no hope.

This is because art and mysticism understand one another. They speak the same language. It is there, at that intersection, that Khalil Gibran will be able to converse with Ghazali; Batman can meet with a strong man like the prophet Moses; the Qur'an can tell us how to watch a movie meaningfully, and prophetic teachings can show us how a visit to the museum may awaken our hidden treasure. This whole affair is nothing but a singularity, and we are all on the same journey towards the summit.

Conclusion

"The Road goes ever on and on,
Down from the door where it began.
Now far ahead the Road has gone,
And I must follow, if I can,
Pursuing it with eager feet,
Until it joins some larger way
Where many paths and errands meet.
And whither then? I cannot say."
– Bilbo Baggins, *The Lord of the Rings*

I first began the journey of writing what has transpired in this book in 2014, at the behest of my friend Saad Omar who asked me to write an intellectual argument supporting the inclusion of the humanities in Islamic seminaries. What unfolded as I began writing my first paper, "The Light of the Blessed Tree: Islam's Intellectual Imperative in Modernity", was what Derrida had emphasized about the power of poetry, its performativity: the ability to convey meaning at primordial levels deeper than grammar.

Like this book, I only had an inkling of what was born through the ink. Once I started writing, I felt a rushing flow of thoughts racing my hands, much like Ruth Stone's galloping horse that could only be caught by the pen if she was quick enough. In this work as well, I cannot recount how many times I was visited by a connection while writing. It requested to be in the show, but then saw how many others had auditioned and left in a blink.

I had the opportunity to workshop "The Light of the Blessed Tree" during my first experience teaching Muslim youth at the inaugural Mishkah retreat in 2015 with Saad Omar. We were both rather apprehensive in the days and months prior to the event due to the metaphysically-rich content of the paper and the fear that it might be too overwhelming for participants who were mostly college and high school students.

What I decided to do then was to follow John Caputo's advice to perceive the divine method as "not an answer but the opening of the question." I transformed each of the nine or so sessions that I taught into a series of queries and left the door of imagination wide open for the students to form their own answers. The screenplay writing advice that my high school teacher and mentor Ryan Goble had taught me many years prior: "Show don't tell" worked wonders during the retreat.

I did not need to explain to students what experiencing *tawhid* should look like in our day and age, only show them the famous scene from *The Empire Strikes Back* when Yoda eloquently describes it for Luke under the guise of the 'force'. Likewise, preparing for death and the afterlife can be gleaned easily through Shakespeare, while leaving oneself open for the unexpected *l'avenir* of divine *qadar* (decree) can be tasted in Derrida's and Caputo's 'opening of the question'.

What inspired me most in the retreat is the diversity of interests and passions. One participant was getting ready to start law school, another an artist, yet another a nurse or engineer. I found out later that the future lawyer was so transformed by the experience that she decided not to go through with her studies and instead started a nonprofit initiative in her community for young people to come together and discuss the meaning of Islam in America. She had reaped fruits from "The Light of the Blessed Tree".

Another moving experience showed me how culture can be a good contagion. During the first week of the retreat, I only taught college students because surely the material was too complicated for high schoolers. A <u>key</u> term from "The Light of the Blessed Tree" that <u>kept</u> circulating among students was Derrida's 'secret attestation', a word that he uses to refer to poetry's unique performative ability.

One day during breakfast, I overheard one high school student tell his friend that pancakes were his 'secret attestation'. It was the <u>best</u> and most <u>blessed</u> gift a teacher could receive, whereby a concept that he helped convey to students was aptly and vicariously translated to the passions of others. I was as happy as Rumi or Ibn al-ʿArabi would be knowing that their teachings are not only benefiting religious devotees, but also nonbelievers. This is about people who may never pray once in their lives but somehow connect with and love these sages. As the prophet ﷺ teaches: "A person will be with those they love."

I introduced chapter two by stating that saints are artists of the soul, while artists are saints at heart. Both seek to find any trace of beauty in the <u>world</u> and magnify that through their work as a way to redeem the <u>words</u> of God from their suffering. It is interesting that both Ibn al-ʿArabi and Ghazali are critical of *ʿulama' al-rusum* (scholars of outer form). Those who are only able to <u>read</u> the body, grammar, and prose of creation, but not <u>tread</u> into its spirit, metaphor, or poetry.

Mark Hederman, an Irish abbot, speaks of the unveiling that artists like Van Gogh received during their lives. They <u>witness</u> and convey with <u>wit</u> what nobody else could understand or appreciate at the time. It is only after their bodily deaths, when the spirit is liberated and free to communicate heart to heart, as Ghazali entrusted in his will, that their works are tasted. The same can be said about many saints, including Ibn al-ʿArabi, who was – and still is – attacked and marginalized by many *ʿulama' al-rusum*, some who even claim to be Sufi but are in reality frightened of both, shore and ocean.

What is intriguing about the term *rusum* is that it is a word that refers to art, specifically drawing. To deprive humanity of spirituality, mysticism, and metaphysics is akin to drawing an outline that lacks shadow, color, or any sign of movement. Incidentally, I've always envisioned al-Junayd's maxim about gnosis: "The color of water is that of the cup" to be similar to children's coloring books that are mere *rusum* (outlines). Then, when you add water, the life dormant in colors emerges.

The scholars of outer form are those who refuse to give thirsty souls the water of life they need. The people who listen to them remain living only in form, but not spirit. Once your focus is restricted to these *rusum*, the outer images, each of which is necessarily unique since as Ibn al-ʿArabi has taught us there is no repetition in creation, the only dimension of reality we are left to perceive is <u>difference</u> without <u>deference</u> and chaos without harmony.

This is precisely why scholars of outer form have no access to the "field beyond belief and unbelief" to which Rumi and other sages have alluded. Ibn al-ʿArabi describes it beautifully in one of his most well-known poems:

> My heart has become accepting of every form
> A meadow for gazelles, a monastery for monks,
> A house for idols, the Kaʿba of a pilgrim,
> The pages from the Torah,
> and leaflets from the Qurʾan.
> I attest to the religion of love,
> wherever its caravan goes.
> For love is my religion and faith.

Nevertheless, some contemporary Muslim legal scholars have actually reached this shore, like the well-known Egyptian polymath Muhammad Abu Zahra, who after mastering the four legal schools of law proclaimed: "I do not walk in the streets of Cairo and see anybody doing anything save that I can find a proof for it in the religion."

Whereas artists and saints are trying to find excuses for beauty to exist, *ʿulamaʾ al-rusum* are only able to tell us where beauty is not, an intellectual inheritance from a negative theology seeking to only <u>define</u> and <u>deprive</u> God of what is <u>naught,</u> <u>not</u> paving the road for an intimate relationship with Him in the very messy contours of existence. For Ibn al-ʿArabi and other Sufi saints, this dissonance between distance and intimacy in our relationship with the divine needs to be theosophically rooted.

There are two ways in which God relates with the world: *tanzih* (transcendence) and *tashbih* (immanence). The first <u>perceives</u> Him as utterly independent and unlike anything in creation, whereas *tashbih* <u>receives</u> the entire universe as nothing but His manifestations. It is neither one of these paths by itself that delivers to perfection and completion, only both at the same time, in perplexity and paradox.

Just as Elizabeth Gilbert expresses that one's art both does and does not matter, so do we find Ibn al-ʿArabi reiterating throughout his writings that the universe is He/not He. It is Him, when envisioned as naught but His manifestations, and not Him because – ultimately – we are nothing … other than Him. And this simultaneous contention between being everything and nothing is where God can be found – as al-Kharraz states – and also where creativity is born.

Without these two eyes of <u>*tanzih*</u> and <u>*tashbih*</u>, <u>*tawhid*</u> is incomplete. One cannot perceive, worship, or love God perfectly without living and tasting the mystery of how He is both distant, yet closer to us than "our jugular vein" (50:16). Why is that so? Because there can be no oneness without multiplicity. As the Sufi teaching says: "Through their opposites are things known." Likewise, *tawhid* can only be witnessed amidst *kathra* (multiplicity), just as He can only be visited at the meeting of opposites.

This transforms *tawhid* into an intimate performance in everyday life. It is all around us, like the force. In his teenage years, Ibn al-ʿArabi migrated with his family from Murcia to Seville. As he traveled through the Iberian countryside, he had his first taste of *sukr* (spiritual intoxication). He witnessed the paradox of change and constancy that permeates nature. In the trees, water, rocks, and grass, just like Yoda had seen … the force is everywhere.

Specifically, it amazed him how a tree constantly changes through the seasons. The cycle of birth and rebirth is incessant. And yet, the trunk and root remain the same. Khalil Gibran noticed the same <u>secret secrete</u> when he spoke of the seasons of the heart. The Sufi mystic, however, witnessed these twin movements of <u>change</u> and <u>constancy</u> as manifestations of the testimony of faith in Islam, serendipitously known as the *kalima* (Word): "There is no god but God, and Muhammad is the messenger of God."

Whereas the first part signals the impermanence of all things since they wither and die, the second calls upon the muhammadan reality, the force that permeates the entire creation and 'creates life', thereby providing whatever sense of stability there is in the world. The first is also a manifestation of *tanzih* since it views eternality and constancy as an exclusive attribute of God, thereby establishing His independence from creation. The second is a vision of *tashbih* that intimates a similar stability between Him and the world, which is – ultimately – none other than Him.

Ibn al-ʿArabi juxtaposes these two visions of *tanzih* and *tashbih* upon the human being as the reflection of the divine image. Just as our likeness in a mirror <u>inversely</u> imitates our movements, so does the human being also refract God in <u>reverse</u>: His manifestations are constantly changing and unfolding, whereas His essence remains immutable. We, on the other hand, <u>stay</u> somewhat the <u>same</u> outwardly, while our inner reality is constantly in flux.

We revisit Eliot's words: "The intersection of the timeless with time, that is an occupation for the saint." Every sense of liminality of which artists speak, being at the threshold of identities, genders, ethnicities, faiths, economic standing, citizenships, crafts, relationships and every other instance of the proverbial fresh and salty water is, as Ibn al-ʿArabi would agree, nothing but different forms of a singular meaning with many *suwar*. All is ultimately rooted in Him.

The artist, like the saint, is perplexed at witnessing these twin movements of *shahiq* (inhalation) and the <u>zephyr</u> of *<u>zafir</u>* (exhalation) that moves the cosmos into ecstasy. In a recent episode of *Doctor Who*, Vincent Van Gogh is brought from his time to the present day so that he can visit an exhibit of his own works. When the doctor asks the curator what he thinks about Van Gogh:

> Well... um... big question, but, to me Van Gogh is the finest painter of them all. Certainly, the most popular, great painter of all time. The most beloved, his command of color most magnificent. He transformed the pain of his tormented life into ecstatic beauty. Pain is easy to portray, but to use your passion and pain to portray the ecstasy and joy and magnificence of our world, no one had ever done it before. Perhaps no one ever will again. To my mind, that strange, wild man who roamed the fields of Provence was not only the world's greatest artist, but also one of the greatest men who ever lived.

As the Qur'an says: "Indeed, you will know its truth after some time." And yet, our human condition is beautifully paradoxical, such that an artist like

Van Gogh who "used his passion and pain to portray the ecstasy, joy and magnificence of the world" should become an embodiment of his own work: the joy that his craft has brought to the world arrives to him only after his passing, at an empty chair where he used to sit.

But perhaps what this episode of *Doctor Who* also shows is that the liberated spirit of the artist can experience its redemption in the here and now, just from the beyond. As Gilbert instructs, your passion is that which you do not need any external motivation to do. Rather, as Norman Mailer had expressed: "Every book I've written has killed me a little bit more." It is the loving annihilation of the artist that should make us cherish them as much as we can, while acknowledging that we will never be able to appreciate what they witness and channel until it is too late.

Such is the cosmic ʿurf, for the glimmer of every star that we witness on a clear night has already perished, with only faint distant memories remaining from its past glory. It is not only Captain Jean-Luc Picard who experienced the joy and agony of people who died thousands of years ago, but also every artist who dreams characters, settings, and worlds into a breath then suddenly awakens from their creative dream. Art is to experience separation continuously and willingly. It is a joyful sacrifice to remind people what it means to be human.

I would like to transition to more pragmatic matters, pertaining to the fruits of the journey undertaken in this book. This work is my constitution in terms of both content and style. It is my constitution since it outlines my creative and spiritual beliefs that govern my life and which I hold so dearly. It is also my constitution in the sense that it embodies all my

<u>senses</u>, how I perceive and engage with the world: a written performance of my bodily journey.

In terms of content, the chapters, paragraphs, and lines of this book are either thoughts that have visited me over the years or were born right before your eyes, in ink on paper. As for style, what has been left unsaid is much more important than the countless words I have exhausted before you. As I outlined in the preface, I have relied upon two techniques to facilitate 'opening of the question'. First, I underlined pairs of homonyms, contranyms, anagrams, alliterations, or terms that seem related in my eccentric imagination. Second, excluding the preface and <u>conclusion</u>, I have <u>included</u> a silent quote on every page of each chapter.

Both the underlined traces and excerpts stand simultaneously within and without the time and space of this work as liminal instances of 'show don't tell'. It is not simply a matter of not having 'room' to explain how each of these examples fit in the surrounding <u>conversations</u>, but more importantly, without your active attempt to 'make <u>connections</u> where none seem to possible or exist', my <u>words</u> would only imprison the possible <u>worlds</u> in your imagination.

I hope that this strategy will make this book a <u>reed</u>-able fertile soil for new flutes every time it is <u>read</u>. For these underlined memories and quotes are only pretending to be written words. In reality, they are prompts, <u>venues</u>, and empty spaces for thoughts to <u>venture</u>. As Ibn al-ʿArabi said in reference to the prohibition against making physical portrayals of the prophet ﷺ or God in Islam: it is not an attempt at iconoclasm, but a struggle to free the imagination. I have also tried to free my readers from the fetters of linguistic chains.

With this in mind, I would like to address the question whether this book is only for artists, meaning those people in society whom we consciously regard as such (e.g., poets, painters, architects, actors, musicians), or everyone else as well, including medical doctors, engineers, businessmen, and accountants. First, I would like to distinguish between the arts and artistry or artisanship, both of which grow from the soil of creativity.

The creative process is not exclusive to artists. It is an imprint in all human beings. If we think of creativity as we have defined it in this book, as the 'translation of the ineffable to the tangible' and 'making connections where none seem possible or exist', then that is as much the brilliance of artists as mothers and scientists. Every human being who has been remembered for some sort of contribution has tapped into their hidden treasure. Thomas Edison, Albert Einstein, and others: without their creative genius, our world would be much different.

I have already spoken about my wife Fatima Nazan whose endearing motherhood continues to be the source of countless creative acts. Our daughter Zahra also exhibits the brilliance of an infant's purity as she draws, sings, or asks questions into being that no adult would contemplate: "Angels like apples", "God loves living in my heart", and "I think the prophet likes candy". You only need to spend a few moments with a child to know that Picasso was right: if only all human beings remembered infancy and lived life creatively through that lens.

In the preceding pages of this book, in each of the four chapters dedicated to the different genres of art: written, visual, auditory, and moving, I simply did not have the space to discuss martial arts, cooking, gardening, carpentry and a slew of other crafts in their proper place. But just as Shahab Ahmed behooves us to regard Islam as a process of making meaning, I also hope each of these four, and other, sections can be viewed not as a final word, but a process and an opening of possible worlds.

Everything we have spoken about regarding the written arts applies to haikus, journaling, and screenplay writing. All that we outlined in the visual arts embraces murals, carpentry, gardening, and cooking. The cadence of our conversation on the auditory arts likewise speaks about musicals, singing, or chanting. Lastly, the moving arts embrace dancing, physical exercise, and any other sense of movement, that most basic reality animating the universe.

What then is the importance of poetry, painting, music, and acting? Their significance is that they are not only self-standing crafts or artforms, but like Shahab's reimagined Islam, also processes. Novels and poetry allude to the importance of witnessing meaning beyond grammar in all crafts. Painting and drawing show us the importance of reading texture and color in all disciplines. Music allows us to witness the rhythm and rhyme that moves the universe. Lastly, acting behooves us to consider the power of being and doing nothing on the stage where mythology is formed and our spirits reformed.

This is exactly why these artforms, together constituting the humanities, have always been considered the cornerstones of humanity and the consciousness of any society and civilization. They are not only *suwar* (images), but also *ma'ani* (meanings). Nurturing the arts in any community leads to artistry and artisanship to thrive therein. Inversely, neglecting the written, visual, auditory, and moving arts will lead to decadence in all disciplines, not to mention religion.

I have often taught that the degree to which a community of faith takes care of its artists is correlated to its spiritual health. In the American Muslim community specifically, as a microcosm of our national educational system, art is perceived as a frivolous hobby. Muslim artists are always underpaid or, even worse, asked to perform freely as charity. It is an unfortunate change of events that a thousand years ago Muslim ruled lands from West Africa to China all had guilds to support artists, while today – even with massive wealth – we refuse to acknowledge these crafts and their sages.

We should become aware, however, that the neglect towards the arts in my community of faith mirrors a national crisis that is tethered to several other trends that define the modernist industrial complex. Rational positivism, the industrial revolution, protestant reformation, and its Islamic counterpart the Wahhabi deformation, have all worked hard to reduce the spirit of faith to its *rasm*: body, grammar and a hollow outline without the holy spirit.

It is not only Wahhabism, but many other reformist mindsets that seek to move Muslims away from what they themselves misunderstood and misconstrued as superstitions that caused the fall of the Ottoman Empire. What that project actually amounted to is a deafening disenchantment of the world and universe. We continue to find the detrimental effects of all of this in almost every Muslim household across America and the world.

If the arts had continued to be <u>supported</u> and <u>sponsored</u> over the past five centuries, then we would have had more Sistine Chapels and Umm Kulthums today than cans of excrement at museums. These artifacts that draw the ire of religious folk highlight the fact that we are missing the real root of the problem: it is the religious folk's own apathy towards the arts that have caused this, so much so that almost no Muslim parent today is willing for their son or daughter to sacrifice a six-digit career as an engineer, doctor, or lawyer to instead become an artist who can bring much needed meditative beauty to our world.

While watching an episode of American Idol, I was humbled by a young Australian musician who willingly left his parents' home as a teenager to become an artist. Although his parents did not stop him from being a musician, he wanted to experience the heartache and struggle of climbing to the summit, which they supported wholeheartedly. He explains how he almost died of hunger, drank water from puddles in the streets and slept backstage in recording studios. But all of this taste amounted to nothing less than him winning the entire competition.

Here, I am reminded of a story by al-Dabbagh about an enslaved man who sought a saint to help free him from his oppressive owner. Some years later, the saint went to the owner and instructed him to free his slave, which he immediately did. The freed man thanked the saint and asked about the reason for the delay in helping him, to which the saint responded: "In order for my words to have any effect on your owner, I had to collect enough money and free a slave myself."

By marginalizing and murdering the arts in our society, we have lost touch with what defines us as human beings. We no longer appreciate love, separation, suffering, or redemption. But we also need to understand that this apathy towards the arts and humanities is not simply the crime of the industrial revolution or the protestanization of Islam under the guise of Wahhabism. Rather, even in some Sufi-oriented segments of the Muslim community, there is a subtle idolization of rational positivism.

The monopoly of the rational disciplines of Islam, especially legal jurisprudence and dialectical theology has not only exiled the way of mystical theosophy, a la Ibn al-ʿArabi, but altogether altered the Muslim consciousness. The constant neural training in religious education to only think in terms of *halal* (permissible) and *haram* (forbidden) has made us forget the ability to venture beyond 'right and wrong', as well as 'belief and unbelief', as Rumi decries.

This lack of aesthetic <u>sensitivity</u> and <u>sensibility</u> manifests in small details, such as the lack of color coordination in our places of worship, carelessness about the 'cultural tongue' in our religious dialogue and sermons, to more serious problems such as the inability to appreciate a song, film, or novel at a level deeper than the superficial criticism of themes that are deemed heretical or musical instruments that are still considered *haram* (forbidden) by many Muslim scholars.

In 2014, I attended a retreat with my friend Saad Omar where he showed an entire Muslim congregation the documentary *Jiro: Dreams of Sushi* about the sage-cook from Japan. Jiro had reached such a summit that he began to hear the siren song regularly in his dreams, gifting him new recipes to use in his restaurant. The farmer who sells Jiro the rice for his sushi tells viewers that there are five-star hotels in Japan who are willing to pay him massive amounts of money for his grain, which he refuses because only Jiro knows how to cook the rice well.

After the documentary was shown, Saad asked attendees about their thoughts, one of whom responded: "These people only care about food like animals" before standing up and leaving. I was disheartened but – unfortunately – not surprised. For this is precisely the legal-<u>prism</u> that has <u>imprisoned</u> the minds and hearts of many Muslims, rendering them incapable of reading beyond the grammar and body of art. This is how they read the <u>words</u> of religious texts and all of God's <u>words</u> as well.

My friend Saad, who has been my visionary companion since the journey of this book began in 2014 with "The Light of the Blessed Tree", is an eloquent antidote to this problem in the American Muslim community. He is an impeccable poet and lyricist whose <u>words</u> bring <u>worlds</u> to life subtly beyond the vale, while paying attention and tribute to the meandering pathways of eloquence in the English language. In his riveting *Swan Song*, beautifully sung by our mutual friend Jawad Mecka, one finds a universal redemption in the souls of many American youth who have been deprived of the <u>breath</u> to <u>birth</u> the precious meanings in their hidden treasure to life:

> *The cemeteries are empty, the movement underground*
> *There is no one left for me, down in Johnson town*
> *I've learned the art of being lonely, just a painting on the wall.*
> *There is nothing you can do for me, leave your flowers and be gone.*
> *And count me with the lost souls, the wayward bound.*

Didn't belong here, don't belong up there.
We'll be the last firefighters in hell.

Saad's written words and embodied Word have inspired countless young Muslims, including another mutual friend, Thalib Razi. Not only a capable musician who brings multiple traditions to life on the oud and guitar, but also more recently an exquisite novelist whose *The Enchanter's Counsel* is a brilliant interweaving of Tolkien's Middle Earth with Sufi poetry and mythology. The hope is indeed there, and I mention it here to <u>augment</u> the <u>argument</u> that human <u>markers</u> like Saad, Jawad, and Thalib are – spiritually – infant-like <u>markers</u> who bring color to the world. They are embodiments of water bringing hued books to life.

Although I myself am a poet and musician as well, I feel the need to emphasize that the method that has unfolded in this book is itself an ancient artform as well. In our hyperspecialized world where we cherish the ability to do only one thing, while being oblivious to how that contributes to our understanding of humanity, the creative ability to 'make connections where none seem possible or exist' across disciplines is a lost commodity.

In *Range: Why Generalists Triumph in a Specialized World*, David Epstein makes the case that focusing on only one craft throughout one's life does not necessarily lead to mastery, at least as much as exploring a wide variety of related paths. What I add here is another dimension, one that does not prioritize the mastery of any single craft as the destination, but rather the 'process of making meaning' itself as the craft and goal. The once celebrated renaissance human, who thought about the overarching questions in life, is dead and needs to be resurrected.

It was a solemn moment during a graduate course, *Theorizing Religion*, when our professor Paul Johnson poignantly pointed that there will never be another Marx or Weber, simply because as a society we no longer prize asking big questions across disciplines. Although I agree that this is the case in the academy, there remains one craft where humanity has allowed itself to tackle those existential dilemmas: the arts. It is Steven Spielberg, Martin Scorsese, John Coltrane, Miles Davis, Yo-Yo Ma, and Krista Tippett who are now challenging religion and the sciences to see each other in the mirror.

This leaves us with a final note on where 'the road goes ever on and on' from here. I only hope that the preceding chapters have been beneficial in one way or another, not only as a source of new knowledge or information, but more importantly as a series of openings of new questions. As I mentioned in the preface, I have intentionally de-academicized this work, choosing not to include an index, footnotes, or list of references despite the numerous quotations and sources used.

I did this because just as our entire psyche changes when we go through the front doors of a museum, allowing our rationality to rest while putting our emotional and creative intelligence to the test, I likewise want readers to feel as though they have entered a museum through the cover of my book. From my experience, footnotes and references simply do not allow our rational fixation to slumber, it keeps lumbering about: whether a statement is true or false or where the proof lies for a conclusion, much like the zealous legalistic mindset that infests the scholars of outer form.

What I have tried to write here is a poetic journey about art and the creative process. I hosted many spirits from past and present whose graciousness I do not deserve, but who continue to be with me as I learn about myself in the process. As I write these final words, I have informed another friend of mine, Joshua Beneventi, an artist who has long since become an embodied art at the summit, that he can be found on every page and within every word of this book.

I also began writing this work shortly after meeting another companion on the road, the consummate actor, martial artist, meditative spirit, and creative soul Ryan Potter; someone whose friendship is a prayer, and so finds himself in all my prayers. Many of the epiphanies in this book have also emerged from my long conversations with the consummate musician Alman Nusrat, an artist who is not only art, but perceives it solemnly everywhere around him. Lastly, I would be remiss to not re-mention my dear brother, friend and mentor prof. Rudolph Ware who graciously wrote the foreword for this book. To all of them I say, you have written my <u>world</u> and now you write these <u>words</u> with me.

What I have shared with you here is only my journey, but I can only be truthful if I <u>speak</u> from the <u>peak</u> of <u>taste</u>, not the <u>paste</u> of somebody else's experience. Since completing my doctoral studies in 2018, I have tried every now and then to publish my dissertation on Jesus in Ibn al-'Arabi's writings, to no avail. It is only when I set out and sailed on the ink of what you see before you that I realized this is what I truly <u>learned</u> and <u>earned</u>. Thank you for <u>reading</u> me and <u>reeding</u> yourself.

252

Postscript: On Being Artificially Intelligent

I thought of writing this short section only after completing the book. I hesitated immensely about stepping foot inside the murky waters of AI-generated art and its place in the grand scheme of metaphysics that I have outlined. However, considering the fact that I am an artist who has a doctoral degree in the humanities and masters in artificial intelligence, I feel compelled to at least express my views regarding this subject, especially in a book about the spiritual foundations of the creative process.

Generally, I am very skeptical of blind hatred of technology, for many reasons. Human beings in every generation have been critical of social changes that occur during their lifetime. When the radio was invented, it was <u>seen</u> as an <u>obscene</u> waste of time. The same can be said about television and video games. More than that, prior to all these inventions, the mass production of books was perceived as an affront to knowledge and the proper etiquette needed to seek it.

And so, I think we should very carefully approach the topic of AI-generated art that has recently taken the world by storm. Of course, it is a development that has been concomitant with other <u>advancements</u> in the world of technology, most especially the <u>advent</u> of the metaverse and widespread use of virtual reality, not only for recreational purposes, but also in medicine and other disciplines.

My concern in the proceeding paragraphs is to focus on AI-generated art in the context of the metaphysical lens we have established in this book. Where do the five levels of being, from *lahut* to *nasut* fit in this new machine-generated art? How does imagination, paradox, and the muhammadan reality engage with this mechanism? Can a machine climb the summit of creativity, from *shari'a* to *haqiqa* like a human artist? Lastly, whether our answer is yes or no to these questions, what ultimately distinguishes a human sage from a robot?

We had recourse to artificial intelligence in some chapters of this book, specifically Steven Spielberg's *AI* and James Cameron's *Terminator 2: Judgment Day*. We highlighted the importance of film, a human technology, as a medium for conveying the ability of machines to display more love and affection for human beings than we can for ourselves. The terminator's sacrifice to save John Connor and a mecca child's ability to seek a motherly love reflect back to us our shortcomings as a species as well as our strengths as artists.

But the underlying movement in films like *AI* and *Terminator 2* is the human artist: directors, producers, set designers, and actors who are able to <u>mend</u> and <u>bend</u> the will of machines to reflect a glimpse of humanity back to the audience. Spielberg and Cameron are masters of *bricolage*, and artificial intelligence was simply one tool among many that they had utilized in the telling of their stories. The same can be said for George Lucas who incorporated advanced technology found throughout galaxies far away in the weaving of mythology in his *Star Wars* universe.

Of course, when one perceives the onslaught of art production coming from the assembly lines of AI-programs, we are amazed by the coordination of colors, shades, and settings that rival the ability of human artists. And yet, as we pay closer attention to human faces and portraits, we notice the absence of life. Sometimes, the machine even reveals its shortcomings and altogether deforms human faces, such that a portrait becomes a horrifying spectacle.

While it is true that even the greatest of portraits painted by human artists are not alive either, there is a subtlety in human <u>art</u> that captures our <u>hearts</u>: the soul of the artist. Let us reminisce on the *Mona Lisa* that remained in the embrace of Da Vinci until his spirit possessed the work. We wonder, what is exactly possessing an artificially generated artwork? Is a simple command sent by a human being to a computer to produce a work of art a sufficient conduit for their spirit to occupy digitized pixels? Who, after all, is the artist here?

I believe that the question whether a machine has a soul and how that affects AI-generated art is a fruitless discussion. Moreover, I actually do not want to spend these last few pages discussing the five levels of being in a machine. Instead, I would like to focus on an overarching problem that concerns AI-generated art: brokenness. All human art has thrived, one way or another, on suffering whence the creative outpouring arrives as a redemption from the artist's inner hidden treasure.

Unlike machines that crash when confronted with an error, we are predisposed to make sense of our faults, even viewing the beauty therein. This much can be witnessed, for example, in the art form of *kintsugi*. One can simply ask whether an artificially intelligent machine would find any utility in intentionally shattering the glass frame surrounding a photograph, as Subotzky has done with his work. Human artists find beauty in brokenness, whereas machines find no utility in that space; this is the dividing line.

Our brokenness is the door to understanding the triumph of the human spirit despite the weakness and temporality of our bodies. In two well-known Sufi teachings, God is first narrated to have said: "All of the sons of Adam are sinners, and the best of them are those who repent", while in the second the prophet proclaims: "If no human beings sinned, then God would bring another creation that sins and repents." The importance of sin here is clarified by the sage Ibn ʿAta Allah al-Sikandari who says: "How much better is a sin that leaves behind humility than a good deed that begets arrogance."

We need to wonder whether a machine can convey this sense of brokenness or choose the path that Abu Nuwwas had taken to live a life of hedonism while simultaneously composing the most heart wrenching poetry proclaiming his repentance; verses that are memorialized to this day. What is the rational and functional utility in committing faults and being reborn, as opposed to just not committing mistakes and accumulating karma points? Can a machine prioritize emotions and feelings into its equations and what do these taste like exactly in wires and binary code?

Let us now contemplate our approach to AI-generated art, taking into consideration the metaphysical foundations in this book. Our reflection here is twofold. First, we pose the same query that we did of 'low' art that belies veils in the translation process: what is the collective human consciousness trying to achieve through this medium, at this point in time?

My answer to this question might appear surprising to some. I believe that AI-generated art is actually our subconscious attempt to better understand, not marginalize, human creativity. This is a journey of othering, of reflecting in the mirror of our own creation, just as God reflects on His names and attributes in our being. However, unlike the divine project, we lack the collective awareness of our own *lahut* to truly appreciate the movements of spirit that animate us and the entire cosmos.

The second dimension requires us to regard AI-generated art as a metaphor that needs to be interpreted, per Ibn al-ʿArabi's advice. As a moment in time, in-between our past and future, what does this phenomenon represent? If the answer to the first question is that human beings seek to other themselves in the mirror of machines, the response to the second query is the reverse: robot-artists reflect back to us our shortcomings. They are indeed a metaphor for our brokenness.

Does this mean that AI-generated art is worthwhile simply because it teaches us about our brokenness? I do not believe so, at least not as long as we insist on approaching this virtual art production as equal to human creativity; a very dangerous prospect. The only path forward, I believe, where AI-generated art can be a fruitful tool in our collective *bricolage* is where we <u>exhibit</u> immense awareness of the metaphor at hand, as we continue to <u>exhibit</u> virtual galleries in pixels.

We have had millennia to inculcate in ourselves the ability to mediate the external *lahut* through human art. We simply cannot approach AI-generated art in the same way, since it does not reflect back to us any sense of soul, suffering, or redemption that beautifully haunts our words, brush strokes, and notes. Instead, we need to internalize this new artificial medium as a broken mirror proclaiming perfection and refusing to acknowledge its faults. If our hands <u>render</u> the <u>tender</u> beauty of our wounds, then a machine's attempt reflects back to us the ego that veils us from our hidden treasure.